# Changing America

## With What " If's "

Timothy J. Amdahl

ISBN:10:-1505404266
ISBN-13:9781505404265

# DEDICATION

I dedicate this book to every American. I hope this book will bring out your patriotic side that so many in our White House and Country have lost. Let's not forget the Minute Men of the past, for someday they may be called upon to return.

# CONTENTS

# ACKNOWLEDGMENTS

I don't in any way wish to solely direct this book in one specific direction, but rather create questions of worthy debate. This book is written with my own opinions, and personal observations. If your name appears, in this book it doesn't make you guilty or innocent, it just means you fall in to the **"What If"** factor.

# CHAPTER ONE

## **The Ferguson Fallout**

I was watching the news one evening, when they interrupted the broadcast, the news reporter started talking about a young black boy that had been shot and killed by a white police officer in Ferguson, Missouri. They had mentioned that the boy was a suspect in a robbery, that he had shop lifted, and strong armed the owner of the store.

The next thing you know, the police officer is suddenly under attack by the **Black Activist,** and the media is on high alert; the truth twisted once again like a callused barbed-wired fence. Then the out of the midst comes the infamous Al Sharpton, flying in with his cape like a superhero to save the day.

**What if** we look at this from the very beginning?

**What if** when the call came in for the police to respond, they would have asked first, which race is he? If he is African American we'll pass, we wouldn't want to racially profile.

**What if** Michael Brown would have never assaulted, or strong armed the owner of the store, and shop lifted in the first place?

**What if** Mr. Brown who was over six feet tall and three hundred plus pounds, would have complied with the officer when he was approached and asked to do so?

**What if** Al Sharpton would have focused on Mr. Browns own behavior of defiance, and lack of respect for authority?

**What if** Al Sharpton didn't really want to wave his cape to save the day, but rather fan the "flame of injustice" for his own personal gains?

**What if** it is Al Sharpton, who is the racist one and not the police officer? Then who becomes the victim?

**What if** all the businesses think twice before building or venturing into certain communities saving them from the arson, looting during the riots, and other serious community problems. What would make a business feel more safe than a church that was under attack by its own community?

**What if** the demonstrations would have stayed peaceful, making it more difficult or noticeable for the looters to steal?

**What if** that was their sole purpose, to find an excuse to justify their own criminal intent to steal and destroy.

**What if** all the store owners would have been sitting in their stores with weapons in hand? Would they not have had a right to protect their property, and themselves in their own stores that they pay taxes on?

**What if** they use black or African American Police Officers to deal with the Black Community, and White or Caucasian Police Officers to handle the White Community? Kind of sounds like segregation, is this where Al Sharpton is heading? What would Martin Luther King think?

**What if** Al Sharpton helped reimburse all the business that were affected by the riots? Let's not forget the police officer who now resigned from his job, for doing his job. Let's see now how the "Help Wanted" section will read.

"Police Officer wanted in Ferguson, MO." I wonder who will apply?

**Faith in our Justice system begins with us.**

## In Ferguson Missouri the lines have been drawn.

Are these lines really about black and white, or are they about the lawful and lawless? What will it take to bring these two forces together to unite as one?

History is a tool we could use to learn from, but who wants to learn and who wants to blame? Let's not face off in violence until we have exhausted all of our other options. Do we not deserve to at least look at all things first? So now who wants to lead this crusade in a positive way?

Where were these people when the stores and businesses were raided and looted? There are two sides to every story the "right side and wrong side".

## <u>Obama's Transparency</u>

"The way to make a **Government responsible** is not simply to enlist the services of responsible men and women or to sign laws that ensure they never stray.

The way to make Government responsible is to hold it accountable. The way you make it accountable is to make it transparent, so the American people can know what decisions are being made, how they are being made, and whether their interests are being well served.

The directives I am giving my administration on, is how to interpret the Freedom of Information Act. For a long time there has been too much **secrecy** in this city.

"Starting today every agency and department should know that this administration stands on the side of not those that seek to hold information, but those that seek to make it known"- Pres. Obama.

**What if** President Obama actually lived up to that which he preached? The above statement was his own words from his own mouth. Yet it is his second term in office, and I have yet to hear of him showing his birth certificate. Is his birth certificate a matter of **national security**? May be it is because when you alter one document to cover a lie, you have to do another one to cover that lie as well, thus creating a chain of events that become continuous. This only makes it harder to find the beginning and the end, or in this case the truth. If nothing else if he could just explain why we don't need to see his birth certificate.

# The Bowing to the King

The day our great, mighty leader The President of the United States approached the King of Saudi Arabia; Pres. Obama bowed holding the Kings hand. Our President appeared **weak and submissive**, not the picture The Ruler of another country wants to make.

**What if** the White House called it what it was, a bow, a kneel, a curtsy, let's just stick with a bow to a King. As Commander and Chief you are there to represent the people of the United States of America. To be President is to be knowledgeable. Our soldiers are warriors that have put their lives on the line for our very freedom. They wear their uniforms with pride and salute as Americans. They do not change their salute depending on the country they are in. The President wears the uniform of the Commander and Chief, therefore he should greet the leaders of other countries as an American, as the Commander and Chief, as our King.

**What if** President Obama would have stood tall looking the King in his eyes man to man? Is that not how we are taught to show respect? The eyes should show the leaders of other countries we mean business. It is time for Americans to stop apologizing for being Americans.

**What if** the bow is a silent message to the King letting him know we will surrender upon his request?

The White House stated that the President was just leaning down because he was so tall. If this were the reason he would have bent at the knees not the waist.

He completely looked down to the ground, again this was a sign of weakness and showing vulnerability exposing his weak side. I know, who am I to question the President of the United States? I am just a natural born citizen who actually has served my country, and protected America through The Dept. of Corrections. You want to see my birth certificate, or my D.D..214?

## Obama speaks on Trayvon Martin

**President Obama's Speech-** "I said when Trayvon Martin was first shot this could have been my Son. Another way of saying that, was Trayvon Martin could have been me thirty five years ago. When you think about why, in the African American Community at least, there is a lot of pain with what happened here. I think it's important to recognize the African American community is looking at this through a set of experiences and history that doesn't go away."

**Pres. Obama states-** "There are very few African American men who haven't had the experience of being followed when in a department store, that includes me." He stated. "There are very few African American men that haven't walked across the street and heard the locks clicking on cars." To me it sounds like the President has issues of his own race.

**What if** he as President is using this as his own personal agenda, like someone else we know?

**What if** I were to bring out the concerns of The American white male who can't relate with walking across the street hearing car doors lock, or being singled out in a department store, or even seeing a woman clutch her purse out of fear because there is a white man present.

**What if** it isn't because they are African American, but because they live in an area heavily populated by criminals?

**What if** they stopped using their race to play victim? Has he or anyone else thought about looking at this as a reason? Race will always be a problem when you choose to use it as an excuse.

## Obama's Promises/Quotes

### Guantanamo Bay
"I will close Guantanamo Bay, and restore Habeas Corpus."- Pres. Obama

### IRAQ
"I promise you if we have not got our troops out by the time I am President, it is the first thing I will do I will bring an end to this war."- Pres. Obama

## US involvement in LIBYA

"We expect this transition to take place in a matter of days and not weeks."- Pres. Obama

## Pres. Obama Personal Statements/Quotes

"I am less interested at passing out blame then I am at learning from, and correcting these mistakes. Where ultimately the buck stops with me."

"My job is to solve problems not to stand on the side lines and harp and gripe."

"I believe marriage is between a man and a woman."

Later he states. "I believe same sex marriages should be able to get married."

The President was asked when congress offers him a Bill, if he promised not to do Presidential signage to get his way?

He stated clearly and immediately "Yes, I believe in the constitution and will obey the Constitution of the United States, and will not use signage statements as away to get around Congress."

Later he states. "I can't wait for Congress to act so where they won't act, I will."

Pres. Obama also states "There are no more Lobbyist. The days of the Lobbyist in the White House are over."

There is a rather large list of names of people who have

accepted jobs in the White House who were Lobbyist, or have close ties to Lobbyist Under the Obama administration.

**Barrack Hussein Obama**, who is he? I know he is called the President of the United States, but where did he come from? Did he grow up here in the United States, or was it another country like Kenya? If it was here, what state was he from? He talks about being Christian, then the next time he talks about how he can relate coming from a Muslim background.

He stated he believed that marriage should be between a man and a woman. I believe this as well, it is because of my religion and faith I believe this; President Obama stated this as well. Then later he stated he believed that same sex marriages should be allowed to get married. I don't believe this, and never will. I would understand if the President stated I don't believe in this, and the only way this would become legal is if Congress or The Senate over ride my vote. But wait the President always has the majority votes right?
He talks about how the Republicans don't want to work with him, but earlier he stated he wasn't going to blame others.

**What if** as President he demanded every politician that is being paid by myself, you, and our neighbors to do a job, to report to work every day until progress is being made.

The definition of progress isn't just smiling at the other party, even though that might be a good start.

It is sitting down to take your job serious, setting goals, and meeting expectations. It is following through completing the tasks at hand.

I understand That it takes more than just the President to get things done, but A President that is a good leader can accomplish much. If you want to be taken serious as President than you have got to take your job serious. If you can't prioritize you show a lack of respect or present yourself as someone not interested in helping America prosper.

## Obama Strokes us off

**President Obama speaks** on the killing of Jim Foley, who was murdered by Isis.

"Today the entire world is appalled by the brutal murder of Jim Foley at the terrorist group Isis.
Jim was a Journalist, a son, a brother, and a friend. He was taken hostage nearly two years ago in Sierra.
Let's be clear about Isis, they have rampaged across cities, and villages killing innocent unarmed civilians, and cowardly acts of violence. They abduct women and children and subject them to torture, rape, and slavery. They murdered Muslims, they target Christians and their religious minorities. Driving them from their homes murdering them when they can, for no other reason than for practicing a different religion.
The United States of America will continue to do what we must do to protect our people. We will be vigilant, and we will be relentless. When people harm

Americans anywhere, we see to it that justice is done."

He states Isis has no place in the 21century. President Obama spoke well of Journalist Jim Foley, and appeared clear on Isis not getting away with the criminal cowardly acts that they have done.

However before Americans can even give him a pat on the back for his strong words and condolences to the Journalist and his family, he is out minutes later seen playing golf. To many of us it was seen as an insincere gesture that his vacation and his recreation comes before our Country and its national security.

I think of the President of the United States as a full time job. There are times you may have to cancel vacations or work a few extra hours at the office. I understand this all too well.

Let me see here, I served my country, two years in the Army and four years in the Marines. I took vacation when I could, and at no time did I ever hold up the "timeout sign" during a crises to go on vacation. Or choose to be on vacation, and not return back to my tour of duty to fight for my country and stand alongside my comrades. I am currently working for the Department of Corrections. I have chosen this career and profession because it is what I like to do. The inmates don't go home on holidays, and they don't get to celebrate their birthdays. This means if they stay in prison we have to have someone watch them. That's me and thousands of other hard working Officers.

When there are riots the Law Enforcement Community comes together to squash the resistance. When there are motorist stranded out in the snow, there are workers out there to help rescue and save them. I think you are catching where I am going with this. If you "sign up" for the responsibility then you should follow it through.

**What if** you would have cancelled your golfing day or your vacation and returned to work early Mr. President, Wow, **What if**?

No one will ever know, because you never did it. I hate to compare Presidents but I am a United States Citizen, and I was a U.S. Marine who's Commander and Chief at the time was Ronald Reagan. I walked tall in my country and He brought out the American pride like I had never seen it brought out before.

Other countries respected us and feared us. There is nothing wrong with them fearing us if they are our enemy. We should be speaking loud and clear if you mess with the U.S. we will see you pay the consequences. America at one time meant something truly strong and powerful, and I believe it will again one day.

**Red White and Blue Represents Freedom not Forgiveness**.

# Hillary fails with Benghazi

The State Department took out thirty plus security personnel from Libya in six months prior to attack. Estimated three to four hundred National Security Officials received State Department E-mails as the Benghazi attack unfolded.

Was information developing, and was the situation fluid? Would we reach conclusions later that weren't reached initially? These were questions asked but never answered.

When asked do you disagree that a simple phone call to those evacuees wouldn't ascertained immediately? That there was no protest, and that specific or key piece of information that could have been easily obtained, within hours if not days was purposefully disregarded. Hillary Clinton Sec. of State's response was She didn't want to look like she was influencing the F.B.I.

**Sec. of State Hillary Clinton**- "We have no doubt, they were terrorist. They were militants, they attacked us, they killed our people, but why and what was going on was unclear. The fact is we have four dead Americans. Was it because of a protest, or was it because some guys out walking one night decided to ambush and kill some Americans? What difference at this point does it make? It is our job to figure out what happened and to do everything in our power to prevent this from ever happening again."

I watched these clips as Hillary was being questioned, examined, interrogated. It made me wonder why she was so mad?

**What if** she felt guilty, because it was her fault?

**What if** when Sec. of State Hillary Clinton made the statement "What difference at this point does it make", her true colors were coming out thinking Americans are disposable.

**What if** when she said It is our job to figure out what happened, and to do everything in our power to prevent this from ever happening again.

Wait, she was being questioned by people who were at the time doing just that. They were trying to figure out what happened so they could hold certain people accountable to see this wouldn't happen again.

Remember I am just your average American tax payer who is watching Fox News, CNN News, along with my Local News. I am only asking the **what "ifs"** to what is being presented to me through the news media.

As Secretary of State, it was her job to protect the people. She is responsible for their safety and their well being. When Hillary went to Benghazi she had the Defense Department preposition assets off the Libyan Coast in case she needed rescued.

**What if** she would have given them the same security that she was so privileged to?

# "No News is Good News"

The news is reported to us not just to inform us, but to influence us as well. If you look at how the news, through the media, helped or hurt the Ferguson riots. It helped some people get new TVs, and other people to take out their anger. It meaning 'the news" brought people together. It also created a lot of property damage, distrust in the community, separation of neighbors, Law Enforcement, other first responders, along with Whites and Blacks.

Yes sometimes the news has that effect. Does that mean we should not report the news? I think if we start from a little circle of truths and work out it, it will be easy to answer. When a family member dies we are all informed not by the news, but by our families and friends. We gather together to show respect and console each other; some members of the families will take it better than others or deal with harsh news better.

Those that can't accept it as easy will have a hard time. It is those that are strong in our families that will lend that extra hug, and console appropriately. They are the ones helping everyone morn together, and share in the grieving process.

The next circle out is when someone in your neighborhood is assaulted or rapped. The local news reports on what they have, to inform the public to be on the lookout for a stranger or a specific person. By having knowledge that a threat is nearby, or possible is "good news".

It is given to help the community be better prepared for a disaster that could happen, and prevent further tragedies. The news is there to inform us and guide us.

**What if** it, the news, didn't exist? How would we look at our country then? Would we still be given the same information? Would we be pushed further away from the truth? Would we then become a dictatorship due to a breakdown in communication?

**What if** the news itself becomes tainted whether by accident or on purpose, then what?


## Killing with Kindness

Are you serious? Hillary Clinton stated that we need to be more understanding of our enemies.
What is it that she wants us to understand about our enemies? Is she wanting us to be caring and forgiving? Is this something we should do before they have surrendered, or wait till they have beheaded a few more Americans?

Is Al-Qaida and Isis going to show leniency to the Americans who's heads they shave, who's hands they bind, who's eyes are blinded, all before they are so inhumanely beheaded?
They talk about how we need to defeat Isis and Al-Qaida. What do they mean when they say defeat them? Do we defeat them by making them give up? Do we exhaust them of all their finances? Do we defeat them by reeducating them on a different way of thinking?

Do we defeat them by having them target someone other than the United States?

**What if** we reeducate Isis and Al-Qaida on the Geneva Convention, oh wait that only applies to war not terrorists. If we are trying to understand terrorists, it should only be for the purpose of where to aim and when to pull the trigger. This is just my opinion as a former U.S. Marine.

## **Celebrity Justice**

Besides Michael Brown and Trayvon Martin, just look at the news. Ray Rice one of the top NFL players is shown over and over again on TV knocking out his girlfriend and dragging her body off the elevator, as he stepped nonchalantly over her body. There was no sign of remorse at anytime shown on the video.

Adrian Peterson the two thousand twelve NFL MVP pleaded no contest to a misdemeanor charge of reckless assault for using a wooden switch to discipline his four year old Son.

Where was Al Sharpton when this black woman was knocked out? Where was he when this young black child was being punished? Would Al Sharpton have been there if this was a woman assaulted by a white male caught on video? What about the four year old? Maybe he is not interested in helping out the black women and children? Maybe Al Sharpton is just being selective in picking and choosing cases?

Does he think this woman's rights were not violated or the child's as well? Here we have four attackers all African American, yet the two that get the attention from Al Sharpton are the black and white, or Hispanic ones. Maybe there are cases out there where he has fought for someone who was attacked by an African American?

In defense of Ray Rice and Adrian Peterson I was not there. Maybe in their cases it is the NFL and other big corporations that are to blame? Think about the amount of money these NFL, NBA, NHL and other superstars get paid and how old are these players?

Are we sacrificing anything for our own entertainment? I think these guys are awesome on the field, but when they are off the field I know nothing about them. I do not want to judge anybody solely on the media, yet I know at times I will as we all will. Whatever happened to just doing your best, and everyone being happy with that? It is all about winning, because winning is making more money and we are all about more money.

We have athletes with their names on thousands of jerseys in all the States and department stores. Why would they not think that they are invincible, or that they may get special treatment because of who they are?

Maybe that's the reason Al Sharpton never showed up? I think sometimes the biggest culprit isn't always the perpetrators, but our media that is quick to jump on these events and topics. If they know people will watch it, they will broadcast it. I think our culture today has lost the value of prioritizing our family morals and values; ratings is how we prioritize.

I love watching the news but even the different networks depending on their beliefs broadcast the news somewhat differently. I do think for the most part they try to be fair and impartial.

If I am wrong on the ratings and prioritizing, then why do we not see more stuff on church events such as church picnics? What about neighbors helping neighbors? You don't see too many school events that aren't sports related. I understand it's a business and if they want to get paid they have to get the audience's attention.

How about reporting on that farmers that put in a hard day's work from sun up to sun set? Or the fishermen or truck drivers that finally makes it home after being on the road or out to sea for days.

I know what you are thinking if it wasn't for the news I might not be writing this book? That is definitely a **what if**.

 Here is a chart just on the NFL. This was information from besttickets.com.

**CRIMES COMMITTED BY NFL PLAYERS SINCE 2000**

| Offense | NUM. of Records | % of Total | Convictions | % Convicted |
|---|---|---|---|---|
| DUI | 185 | 27.82% | 152 | 82.16% |
| Assault | 90 | 13.53% | 55 | 61.11% |
| Drugs | 84 | 12.63% | 57 | 67.86% |
| Domestic Violence | 76 | 11.43% | 38 | 50.00% |
| Alcohol Related | 52 | 7.82% | 32 | 61.54% |
| Driving Violations | 37 | 5.56% | 28 | 75.68% |
| Weapons Violation | 37 | 5.56% | 25 | 67.57% |
| Other | 26 | 3.91% | 18 | 69.23% |
| Disorderly Conduct | 13 | 1.95% | 6 | 46.15% |
| Sexual Assault | 12 | 1.80% | 7 | 58.33% |
| Theft | 11 | 1.65% | 6 | 54.55% |
| Traffic Warrants | 6 | 0.90% | 4 | 66.67% |
| Animal Abuse | 5 | 0.75% | 4 | 80.00% |
| Manslaughter | 5 | 0.75% | 5 | 100.00% |
| Hot Checks | 4 | 0.60% | 3 | 75.00% |
| Obstruction of Justice | 4 | 0.60% | 1 | 25.00% |
| False Info on License | 3 | 0.45% | 2 | 66.67% |
| Probation Violation | 3 | 0.45% | 3 | 100.00% |
| Burglary | 2 | 0.30% | 1 | 50.00% |
| Failure to Appear | 2 | 0.30% | 2 | 100.00% |
| Murder | 2 | 0.30% | 0 | 0.00% |
| Soliciting a Prostitute | 2 | 0.30% | 2 | 100.00% |
| Stalking | 2 | 0.30% | 1 | 50.00% |
| Window Tint Violation | 2 | 0.30% | 2 | 100.00% |
| Total | 665 | 100.00% | 454 | 68.27% |

## Michelle Obama interviewed

When Michelle was asked on what was going on when her husband was trailing Hillary Clinton forty six percent to thirty seven percent in the African American community Michelle said. "First of all that's not going to hold, I'm completely confident black America will wake up and get it. What we are dealing with here is the natural fear of possibility. When I look at my life, the stuff we're seeing in these polls has played out my whole life.

I have always been told by somebody that I'm not ready, I can't do something, my scores weren't high enough. There's always that doubt in the back of the minds of colored, people who have been oppressed and haven't been given real opportunities."

Well I am not sure here but why do we ask questions about black communities? I guess it is so we have a better understanding of what they are thinking. She stated she had complete confidence in the black community.

If this is so why does she need for them to wake up? Aren't they already supposed to be awake? Shouldn't they be taking the presidential election seriously? She states we are dealing with the natural fear of possibility. When I buy a lottery ticket I fear the loss of the dollar but then there is hope that out shines fear. It tells me there is always that one slight chance I might be the winner. If you fear possibility then you don't understand it.

Now let us look at what has played out in Michelle Obama's life." I have always been told by somebody I'm not ready." This sounds like me I had been told before I couldn't do a lot of things, including joining the Marines. You know what, I never played victim. I did what many said I couldn't. I over came, adapted, and improvised.

Michelle stated her scores were too low. I was an average to less than average student in school.

I don't look back and blame my race because I was not applying myself like I should have, but instead I look at if I could have done it over, I would have worked harder and asked more questions.

Michelle Obama speaks about the doubt that is in the back of the minds of colored people, who have been oppressed and haven't been given real opportunities. Who is she to talk about being oppressed? If she was oppressed then her theory on not being given opportunity just collapsed. I haven't yet been to the White House, or made triple figures, or have my own secret security detail.
I'm not being watched by the media because of who I am. I have been on CNN, but it was not because I was the topic, but rather the Commander Six Fleet Strike Force South Southern Europe. Admiral Martin a highly decorated naval officer who was the topic of the news during a change in command ceremony. I just happened to be one of the few Marines that were blessed to serve on his security detail, serving two years with the Admiral who was highly loved and respected by most. The **what "Ifs"** are shrouded here by race, wealth and religion.

## How does Michelle view the poor who are not black? Are they not seen as oppressed as well?

Let us look at our fifty states and how they rated on poverty.

# Very High Level of Persons Below Poverty Level

- 1. Mississippi - 21.2%
- 2. Arkansas - 17.3%
- 2. Louisiana - 17.3%
- 2. Kentucky - 17.3%
- 5. New Mexico - 17.1%
- 6. West Virginia - 17.0%

# High Level of Persons Below Poverty Level

- 7. Oklahoma - 15.9%
- 8. Texas - 15.8%
- 9. South Carolina - 15.7%
- 9. Alabama - 15.7%
- 11. Tennessee - 15.5%
- 12. Montana - 14.8%
- 13. Arizona - 14.7%
- 13. Georgia - 14.7%
- 15. North Carolina - 14.6%
- 16. Michigan - 14.4%

# Median Level of Persons Below Poverty Level

- 17. Oregon - 13.6%
- 18. New York - 13.6%
- 19. Ohio - 13.4%
- 19. Missouri - 13.4%
- 21. California - 13.3%
- 22. Florida - 13.2%

- 23. Indiana - 13.1%
- 24. Idaho - 12.6%
- 25. South Dakota - 12.5%
- 26. Maine - 12.3%
- 27. Illinois - 12.2%
- 28. Pennsylvania - 12.1%
- 29. North Dakota - 12.0%
- 30. Rhode Island - 11.7%
- 31. Iowa - 11.5%
- 32. Colorado - 11.4%
- 33. Nevada - 11.3%
- 33. Kansas - 11.3%
- 33. Washington - 11.3%
- 36. Nebraska - 10.8%
- 37. Vermont - 10.6%
- 38. Wisconsin - 10.4%
- 39. Virginia - 10.2%
- 40. Massachusetts - 10.0%
- 40. Delaware - 10.0%

## Low Level of Persons Below Poverty Level

- 42. Minnesota - 9.6%
- 42. Utah - 9.6%
- 44. Wyoming - 9.4$
- 45. Connecticut - 9.3%
- 46. Hawaii - 9.1%
- 47. New Jersey - 8.7%
- 48. Alaska - 8.4%
- 49. Maryland - 8.1%
- 50. New Hampshire - 7.6%

This information came from http://usliberals.about.com.

If you look at the states that have the highest rate of poverty, you will see most are the southern States or warm States, with the exception of Michigan which ranked sixteenth.

I'm not sure if that means anything more or less, unless maybe in the cold States people may feel they have to work just due to the environment they are in.

## <u>NYPD assassination</u>

December twentieth two thousand fourteen at around three p.m. two New York police officers assassinated while sitting in their car. My heart goes out to them, and to their families. When they walked out their door early that morning to serve their community, few knew what to expect.

The officers know all too well what is out there, yet they continued on to their tour of duty. To provide safety and security, to protect and to serve. Being a police officer isn't a job that is usually appreciated, in fact they are usually set to higher than normal expectations and quickly scrutinized when they make a human error.

The communities often appreciate them but there are some communities that take them for grant it. Again two police officers killed by an African American gang member who then took his own life. The news reported that it was in retaliation over the Michael Brown shooting and the Eric Garner death by a police officer.

Rev. Al Sharpton expressed his concern quietly asking for peace, yet there was support on his side for retaliation towards the police.

**What if** Al Sharpton would had done that in the Ferguson shooting? Today in the news they mentioned Michael Brown as a young unarmed black man. Let's get real here, he was over three hundred pounds. He was hardly unarmed when you out weight someone by a hundred pounds at minimum.

Law enforcement is trained to use deadly force as a last resort. We have to trust in our police officers enough to allow them to do their job for our safety. Sure there are going to be times that there is corruption but if we use the law of the land in serving justice and not five hundred people out looking for a reason to get a new television or burn down a neighborhood.

Posy's are the thing of the past. Don't take the law into your own hands, use the courts. When we look at the video of the police officers struggling  with a citizen on the Brooklyn Bridge you will see many people walking following them as they are struggling, but no one is helping either one of them, Why? You can hear a woman in the background shouting keep filming.

**What if** these people instead of standing around filming they assisted the officers?

**What if** they were looking, hoping for another statistic? What is it that makes people want to watch others get hurt?

Maybe it is just certain people of a certain culture or maybe it is criminals themselves hiding right inside these crowds making them look more like mobs.

Law enforcement will always have a battle on their hand especially in the bigger cities when it comes to fighting crime, but the rest of us should be seriously asking ourselves what did we do to help the officer.

## Sony ready action cut

When our entertainment community is threatened by another country, for example North Korea, or any other country. Whether we are talking guns and missiles, chemical warfare, or a sophisticated virus launched through the internet to cause havoc and or chaos. We must take it serious. Sony chose not to play the movie, *The Interview*.

**What if** they did? How would we respond? I know some think Sony should not submit to the demands of the cyber tyranny. Anytime a country chooses to attack the United States of America to produce harm and interrupt our flow of life and stability. They should be handled swiftly and efficiently so that all countries know the consequences for doing so.

**What if** our president made an example out of North Korea?

**What if** he actually followed through with what he said he's going to do? President Obama spoke tough on Isis and then went right out playing golf. He talked about possible consequences on the cyber threat, then left to go on vacation with his family. How much vacation does the President get a year? Maybe he writes in his own vacation as needed.

**What if** a firefighter used his vacation only during times he was needed most? How many lives and structures would be lost?

Why is it when a crisis appears the President seems to run the other way? It is possible I might be misreading our President. Remember I am just bringing out the **what "ifs".**
Former President Jimmy Carter excused President Obama for not showing up in Parris, France for the rally against radical Islamist stating he understood what it is like getting back after vacation. I'm not sure here but is anyone else seeing a behavioral pattern here?

I wonder if Presidents cover for each other like we do at our work place? I wonder if Jimmy Carter and President Obama are both southern boys?

**What if** President Obama took advice from the other retired Presidents, or would he feel like he was being insulted?

**What if** he swallowed his pride for the betterment of our country

# <u>Americans</u>

Let justice be served in fairness

As the media brings out awareness

For no one shall be above the law

Let not the truth be edited but be raw


For what was, is and what is, was

Let no excuse be just because

But rather let us all unite

As Americans let's do what's right

# CHAPTER TWO

## <u>Attorney General goes rouge</u>

Eric Holder Is the Attorney General. He spoke about the injustice to the citizen by the law enforcement community. He stated the police were far too aggressive. He is a leader in a position to make calm, but chooses to provoke and entice rage along with violence through stupidity and or ignorance, in the communities that need law enforcement the most.

**What if** they stop labeling all cops as bad, or all African Americans as victims?

**What if** we call a young unarmed African American that's over three hundred pounds, who's committed a crime a criminal? Trayvon Martin was identified as a young black male as well. When the media talked about him, they showed pictures of him in his younger days. Why not show pictures of him for who he is, rather than who he used to be?

It only makes the media look tainted in order to influence the vast majority of people into sympathizing for the ones who are the criminals.

The media reported that the killer to Trayvon Martin was white, only to be later identified as Hispanic. They still tried to attach this as a hate crime white on black which it was not.

The media needs to be sure on what it reports, to ensure it is accurate. Like I said earlier I believe most the time they do, but there are times information gets passed wrong.

Mayor De- Blassio is another important character that had the ability to quell his community, yet chose to turn his back on his own law enforcement agency for reasons unknown. He told his officers to sit back and not to respond on the bridge. To let one person break the law is unacceptable, to let a mob is nothing more than willful neglect and dangerous. We need to enforce the laws not bend them.

Why don't we get Eric Holder, President Obama, mayor De-Blassio, and Al Sharpton together and see if they could tell the police when to intervene. Maybe they could tell the police how and when to use deadly force. I would like to know their answers, maybe they have some better solutions that we are not aware of.

It appears our President wants to divide our nation by black and white, rather than unite it as one red, white and blue country.

It is easy to say we have problems and we need to fix them, but none of these leaders have gone in detail to explain what is wrong in specific.

Let us look at Michael Brown. What did the police officer do that was wrong? When should he had pulled his gun? Please oh great leader walk us through how this could have and should have been handled? If you can't, why not? How about Al Sharpton what is your solution in detail?

I'm sure they will talk their way around the topic passing blame on anybody and everybody. They are not looking for the truth, they are seeking their own outcome to their own justification of racial retaliation. Martin Luther King JR. would be disappointed in the way they have taken advantage of racism in our society

## **Prison u turns**

Have you ever sat back and wondered about how prisons operated, when it comes to releasing inmates? Prisons are filled daily with murderers, gang members, drug dealers and users, child molesters and many other assorted criminal elements. Once they get incarcerated they are set to do a certain amount of time and then many get released early on parole. Many have to go back to the same community they were arrested in to finish out their parole. Some may think that the person who just was released maybe set up to fail. He is after all going back to an area where he will be surrounded by those that supported his negative behavior in the first place. So let us ask the **what if** question.

Would you want one of these criminals to live near you? If we broke up these criminal communities would they then stay separated, or would they find ways to congregate till they became a new criminal community networking its crime strategies spreading crime like a malignant cancer?

Keeping them all in their communities is what many of the inmates that get released want. It is where they grew up, where their roots and history are. Many want to stay near family, I can easily understand that. I would love nothing more than for my whole family to live nearby so I could spend time with the ones I love.

**What if** these families united and stood against the gangs?

**What if** they united to build factories and encourage growth and an honest trade.

**What if** the communities would shun gangs while supporting the youth of tomorrow?

### To build a community, one must own it.

# From the Bureau of justice statistics in 2005

- About two-thirds (67.8%) of released prisoners were arrested for a new crime within 3 years, and three-quarters (76.6%) were arrested within 5 years.
- Within 5 years of release, 82.1% of property offenders were arrested for a new crime, compared to 76.9% of drug offenders, 73.6% of public order offenders, and 71.3% of violent offenders.
- More than a third (36.8%) of all prisoners who were arrested within 5 years of release were arrested within the first 6 months after release, with more than half (56.7%) arrested by the end of the first year.
- Two in five (42.3%) released prisoners were either not arrested or arrested once in the 5 years after their release.
- A sixth (16.1%) of released prisoners were responsible for almost half (48.4%) of the nearly 1.2 million arrests that occurred in the 5-year follow-up period.
- An estimated 10.9% of released prisoners were arrested in a state other than the one that released them during the 5-year follow-up period
- Within 5 years of release, 84.1% of inmates who were age 24 or younger at release were arrested, compared to 78.6% of inmates ages 25 to 39 and 69.2% of those age 40 or older.

**Let's stop recidivism, let's break the cycle**

# **Ferguson Missouri's neighboring town**

In Berkeley Missouri a suburban police officer shot and killed a man that pointed a gun at him. Berkeley is a neighboring town of Ferguson Missouri, where Michael Brown was killed in August. According to the St. Lewis county Police spokesman, the officer was conducting a routine police check at the gas station. When the officer approached two gentleman, one of the men pulled a gun and pointed it at the officer. The officer fired several shots, striking and fatally wounding the one, the other one ran off, but they did retrieve the gun.

This is becoming a daily thing. Someone might argue and say the officer approached those two guys because they were black, but once they pulled a gun they became criminals. I know I have covered a lot of this already, but I want you to see this is not an isolated incident. Police officers all over are having to not just watch the criminals but the politicians who have recruited citizens to speak for them. The problem is their voice is being heard in gunshots.

If people are so unhappy here in this country and they feel they are not being treated fairly, they have two choices use the courts to change things appropriately, or **what if** they leave our country. If there is another country that will treat you better than go. I'm sure you are not that unhappy.

We have thousands of illegal immigrants in this country. Why do you think they are here?

**What if** we asked each one do you want to live here or go home, which do you think they would choose? I will be the first to say there are many areas in this country that could use some attention.

**What if** we use our adult skills and  create organizations and committees to address these problems, not with blame but solutions.

## Immigration saturation

We are looking at ways to make our country great, but yet we take a blind eye at some of the obvious things. If we look at unemployment for example.

**What if** we kicked all the illegal immigrants out of this country just to start with. How many jobs would we have available for our legal citizens? If they were legal we could collect taxes from them and they could help support the communities they live in?

**What if** we look at how many that are illegal break the law? Why do you think they break the law? Some do, because they can't get real jobs because then they would be captured and deported, well that is what is supposed to happen.

**What if** some of the illegal immigrants use their invisibility to their advantage to purposely go undetected while all the time continuing to commit crimes against you and I?

We get these immigrants in our country committing crimes and when they get caught they think they should be given free representation, in other words they are wanting you and I to pay for their attorney.

**What if** we went back to kicking them out when they get caught?

**What if** we did not reward them with our privileges, such as the right to vote, drivers license, or a legal State I.D.

**What if** our president and the rest of the politicians got serious with this? Just because it gets brought up here and there does not mean it has been properly addressed.

**What if** one of the requirements be they learn to speak our language to become a citizen?

### Welcome to America please fill these out

The information that has been obtained here came from the following web site.
**http://www.dhs.gov/sites/default/files/publications/ois_rfa_fr_2013.pdf**

According to this web page under homeland security, there were 69,909 persons admitted to the United States as refugees during 2013. There were 25,199 individuals granted asylum affirmatively by the Department. of Homeland Security. There were 9,933 who were granted asylum defensively by the Department of Justice.

Documents for travel to the United States were issued to 13,026 individuals who were approved for derivative asylum status while located abroad. There were 2,240 individuals approved for derivative asylum status while residing in the United States.

The first refugee legislation in the United States was the Displaced persons Act of 1948, which brought 400,000 Eastern Europeans to the United States. There was also the Refugee Relief Act of 1953 and the Fair Share Refugee Act of 1960.

The above web site can give you additional information with a variety of different charts.

These are just the numbers of those that came in legitimately. To all those that are illegitimate either turn yourself in and register and help out the communities you live in or return to your country and give some other person an opportunity to come here legally. I am just voicing my opinion again, but **what if** we followed through?

## Illegal Immigrants!
## Uncle Sam wants you to register.

# __The first Amendment__

## Amendment 1

Congress shall make no law respecting an establishment of religion, or prohibiting the free exercise thereof; or abridging the freedom of speech, or of the press; or the right of the people peaceably to assemble, and to petition the government for a redress of grievances.

The riots that took place in Ferguson, did not fall in under this amendment, because there was no peaceable protest. Once they shouted words of violence "Burn this bitch down" and they broke windows and doors, robbing and looting, burning buildings, whether due to rage or just for fun they at that time lost their right to assemble.

We look at the first amendment and we can look at our President and see how he has allowed our rights to be violated. Isn't the taking away of a bible or the ten commandments sign from the White House a violation of those who believe in the bible? What about the pledge of allegiance in schools. Are the schools not only violating the rights of religion, but also censoring a part of history that so many of us were taught. In history classes, do they talk about America with pride, or are they ashamed of who we are and how we got where we are today? Have we become so sensitive that we have people offended by a tree called the Christmas tree?

They want to be politically correct by just calling it a holiday tree. What holiday are they celebrating? This is one example showing how our politicians try to please as many as they can rather it is right or wrong.

We need leaders that are not afraid to take a stand. It is just like the example I used earlier of the president, stating He believed marriage was between a man and a woman then he said he thought same sex marriages should be allowed to get married. Maybe he was thinking of Michelle on the one and Michael on the other one?

I believe everyone should be allowed to practice their own religion, as long as it doesn't cause harm to someone else. It seems we are selective when it comes to when we use our religion. When a person goes to court they are told to raise their hand and swear on the bible to tell the truth, the whole truth , so help you God. When we work and collect pay checks or go buy and sell items, no one is saying I won't take that money because it says in God we trust on it. If you were truly against God you would not and could not buy, sell or barter with money that had Gods name on it.

I am able to talk here about religion because it is my first amendment right. I just have to make sure I do not offend anyone in a manner that would infringe on their rights. Again I am not trying to direct you in any certain path, but rather get you thinking about your rights.

Your choices are yours to make, but it's nice having information brought out that makes you ask **what if**?

**What if** the next thing they try and take is God's name out of the dictionary because it offends somebody. Our country was founded on freedom. Do you think our country was stronger when God was included rather than excluded? In the Marines we were taught the order. God, Country, Corps. That was and is our order of faith and loyalty.

## Pastor Wright preaches

I watched some of the Reverend Wright's sermon on a you tube video. I listened openly and objectively, wanting to understand his way of thinking. Some I agree with and most I didn't. But his beliefs are his to own and share as he likes.

 I believe that God is who he is and he will not change as well. I believe that it is not God that should change, but us.

**What if** we do not forgive those who condoned slavery, are we no better off than them? Does God not tell us we are to forgive all? I get from the reverends sermon to hate those who are white because of what they did in the past. I am not for slavery and I think every U.S. citizen should be treated and respected. I don't care if you are black, native American, Jewish. or Mexican. Americans should stand united not divided. I think if you are able to work you should. The Reverend Wright talked about how we killed thousands, in different battles and took from the Indians and brought blacks over from Africa. The question here is what do we do from here?

What does the Reverend want our next move to be? I think history speaks for itself. We can learn from it, or ignore it. The **what "if's"** are important.

**What if** we try to learn from our past. By questioning those we do not believe in. We still need to look inwardly, to challenge our own inner selves. The one thing I will say about the Reverend is he doesn't appear to try and hide himself in a fictitious manner. Remember freedom of religion falls in under the first amendment. Let us show respect to the first amendment in the Bill of Rights and all those who wish to use it to its full advantage.

**To express oneself is your right**

# The second Amendment

### Amendment 2

A well regulated militia, being necessary to the security of a free state, the right of the people to keep and bear arms, shall not be infringed.

There is no if, and, or but, in the above amendment. We Americans have the right to bear arms. There are some that have committed crimes that have lost their rights, but to the law abiding citizen who faithfully follows their State and country's laws they have the right to bear arms. I hope we don't take our rights for grant it.

**What if** our country secretly tried manipulating events so as to gain control of all our weapons?

 **What if** they were right now buying up all the ammo for a future event? Remember I told you some day that the minute men of the past may be called upon to return and fight for our country like never before. Maybe they know this and are trying to cut us off at the pass so we will not have the weapons or ammunition needed when the time comes? Why are there some politicians that are against conceal carry yet they either are carrying or have security that is carrying, protecting them?
The N.R.A. is out there fighting for us.

 **What if** they didn't exist? Would our Government be even more blatant?

Some people don't want their guns taken from them, but don't see an issue with others losing their rights. Just because they don't feel a need to carry concealed, or to protect ones person or property. If you give the Government an opportunity to divide us gun owners then you weaken a strong union.

## Guns don't kill they protect

# **Term Limits**

I think many Americans believe that our politicians are more interested in securing a safe, secure and lucrative benefits package that provides all of them with their basic extravagant high end style of living, while the rest of us suffer, scrape and manipulate our finances to accommodate our own basic needs for survival.

**What if** the politicians were set up on the same retirement system that our military was on?

**What if** our politicians actually had to work a real job? I wonder how many have had real jobs or served in the military? I wonder how many have chose to ignore what they believe in, so as to make some one of more power and authority happy in hopes for a future promotion for themselves?

**What if** we had term limits for all political positions? Is it fare that our politicians can get guaranteed benefits with hardly doing any time, or hardly doing any work? Our military warriors, Sons and daughters are on call every day and will travel to where ever our country needs them to go.

**What if** nothing else they get a benefits package that is as lucrative as our prestigious politicians? I would much rather pay the guy with the gun protecting me from our enemies, than a politician who will only pick up a pen to sign something that benefits him or a select few.

I remember when we had a State Representative come speak on the behalf of our State benefits and the violation of our State contract. He was clear on agreeing we were getting screwed by the Governor who did not follow through on his part of the contract, but without making it official. He admitted his hands were somewhat tied due to how the districts were set up giving him less authority.

He was still a politician and would not speak on his actual views when asked, but instead stated he was just here to collect everyone's perspective and concerns with issues.

I know I sat back smiling thinking, at first he seemed genuine but then deceptive as he twisted words and meanings around so as to be taken in multiple ways. In some ways I liked that he was not just deceptive, but openly impartial. He was not shy on letting everyone know he wasn't going to take aside. I respected him for at least being honest enough to say for political reasons I can't at this time agree or disagree.

**What if** family members couldn't directly take the same position that had been previously held by anyone directly related to them? An example might be Hillary Clinton running for president when her husband had already held this position. It is a perfect example of term limits being manipulated by name only. Do you think that Bill Clinton wouldn't have any influence on Hillary, or the presidency?

Would this not be a version of an extended term in office? Would this not give Bill Clinton a chance to break in a new intern?

**What if** we move on to a new generation of elected officials.

**What if** we had more control on ousting those that don't live up to our standards of conduct?

**What if** we used the check and balance system to benefit our country, instead of using secret deals hidden in layers of, if, and, or, buts written in codes of big words and legal jargon specifically used to confuse the masses.
**What if** after two terms they had to move on? Do you think they might then look out for others as well?

## Owning responsibility

Our we living in a time where everyone is held accountable for their actions? We have Susan Smith that killed her kids driving in to the river. She then lied about it making the community look for a suspect that didn't exist, actually the killer did exist. She was the killer everyone would soon find out about.

There was Tina Lopez who was accused of suffocating her two year old daughter.

In two thousand and fourteen A mother starved her nine month old child so she could pay bills. She paid the internet and net movie channels, along with the TV bill. She allowed her nine month old to starve only getting up to seven pounds

These are just a few of the many horrific examples that are out there. We have these people who are given a position of power, not through us but from their own families and upbringing. Are they to be held accountable for their actions of neglect and willful abuse due to their own selfishness? Are we supposed to understand and enable, judge or patronize, or just forgive and forget?

**What if** we made these people die the same death that they gave to their victims? Would these people all think twice about their actions? I'm sure this sounds brutal and barbaric, but you can't say it wouldn't make you ponder a moment before committing these horrific acts of violence. Let us look at another example of responsibility. When children and their parents go to school to register they get handed the school handouts and other normal papers that all go hand in hand with registering, but there is one paper they seem to have added since I was in school, it is the supply list.

I think it is here that I have to ask about why are we, the responsible parents having to pay for the other kids school supplies? Am I being selfish, or am I seeing free hand outs to other parents that are not responsible with their money?

Like the mother that chose to starve her nine month old so she could play and squander her money. When we pay for the other kids supplies I know it is so that they are not humiliated, but are we not enabling the parents that know someone else will care for the educational needs and expenses of their child?

I look at kids coming home with ten times more homework than I had when I was in school. The kids are sometimes not even able to get all their books in their backpacks. I wonder if the teachers are just going over everything rapidly and sending home their school work for the parents to help finish? I also sat back thinking about when I was in school, which was a very long time ago. I do think the kids of today are far more advanced than I was at their age. So I do think the teachers are doing a great job.

I was at a school event a few weeks ago when I watched a mother with her three kids and the grandmother was there as well. The mother couldn't control her own children, she pawned her young son off to her daughter who wasn't much older. It is sad to see a mother who was more interested in her own needs than her children's. It took the grandmother with her years of experience and maturity to guide and calm the children. The mother was not appreciative at all and acted as though that was her moms responsibility. It is these times I ask myself if we are truly helping or hurting?

### Enabling only serves as a crutch.

## **Equal Rights**

We talk about having equal rights for all. That means that all rights should be equal for everyone and not just the minorities.

So when does equal no longer mean equal? When you apply for some jobs you will find that whether you are applying to get your foot in the door, or you are already in and you're going for a promotional interview, that some jobs give you extra points. If you are a certain race you may get a few points. If you are a female, or prior military you could get points If you have an education or work experience these give you points as well.

Do these points not give an unfair disadvantage to your typical white males? How do you make it equal for a white male who goes up against a female or some other race? I think if they have an educational back ground, or prior military, or work experience then that is fine and fair. But to get points for just being born of another color or sex than I think equal has lost its true value. What about being qualified for a particular job? With work experience you might be qualified by having actual hands on experience. With an education you could be qualified through knowledge and practical exams. If you are prior military you earned the points by putting your life on the line for your country, that's the least they can do for you.

**Equal, being the same in quantity, size degree, or value.**

Let us look at equal in the military for example. If I worked side beside with a female in the military in a combat zone, I would feel it was my duty to protect her. I am sure she would be offended by this statement thinking I thought less of her. The truth is I am just thinking the way I had been raised and what has been bread in me through generations. Men now were once boys who were taught to be nice to girls, don't hit them and always stand up for a girl getting picked on. These were traits taught by our families, our teachers, our ministers and other adult role models

If we look at TV we can see on that television reality show Survivor that all you have to do is look at how the women use their charm and beauty to manipulate and deceive, causing friction between factions, even in their own tribes. Sure the guys do it as well, but this is what could easily happen in the real units where life and death really matter. Men think a certain way and are able to desensitize horrible and gruesome acts of violence in a time of crisis. Having a woman in the midst does change the simple things like, what you talk about when they're around. Where to go to the bathroom, or showering.

Let's look at another situation that actually happened. Five other soldiers were captured and subsequently rescued 21 days later. Jessica Lynch was serving as a unit supply specialist with the 507th maintenance company. Their convoy was ambushed by Iraqi forces during the Battle of Nasiriyah

They were rescued on April 1, 2003. Why is it there were five rescued, but only her name gets mentioned? Were the other soldiers not any more victims or heroes than she was? Did they not have families that worried and wondered on their demise? I guess they were not equal?

## **Pro Life or Pro Choice**

I believe our country has way to many activist. Everyone wants to pander to something. Let us look at abortion, here we have two groups of people that have legitimate arguments on both sides. Let us look at this from the Pro life side first.

They believe abortion is murder and that you are killing a living breathing child. I can't argue on this, because I believe that they are as well, however is this embryo, or fetus able to feel emotion, or pain? Is this the reason they are against abortion, or is it because they are ending a life before it gets started? It could be due to their religious beliefs, which this by itself makes a strong argument.

Who are these people that are pro life? Are they women, men, are they rich, or poor? Are these people, family orientated, or do they come from broken families? Are they Republicans, or Democrats, do they work or are they well fare recipients, or does any of this even matter?

Let us look at the other side, those that are pro choice. This group understands that a life is involved in the realm of politics, however the life they are fighting for is not that of the embryo, or fetus, that has yet to breath this earthly air, but the life of the mother whose only focus is to do what is right, or in the best interest of her and or the child. Once again we have to look at who these people are on both sides to evaluate their motives as well.

They believe the decision should be left to the mother and not other people, or the government which continually tries to interfere in family values challenging our moral ethics.

**What if** those that are pro life volunteer to help feed these babies, or change their diapers?

**What if** they offer their time, to comfort these children?

**What if** we get real. How many that are out there petitioning for pro life would be willing to go care for a child that they protested be saved from an abortion? How many babies have grown up without one, or both of their parents?

**What if** the mother isn't able to financially or emotionally take care of the child? What should happen to the child then?

**What if** the child's parents were Susan Smith, or Tina Lopez, knowing the horrific tragedies that the children went through would you still be pro life, or would you make an exception in those type cases?

**What** if the baby was going to be born blind or mentally challenged knowing this ahead of time would you still feel the same way?

**What if** a woman was raped?

**What if** she can't stop reliving the traumatic events of that situation because every time she looks her baby in the eyes or hears her baby cry, or scream it brings back painful memories. This would push her, or could push her away from bonding with the child, which is an important part of motherhood.

**What if** instead of focusing on some other woman and her embryo slash fetus, we focus on pro adoption? Here you can take charge and save the life of a child that already is living and breathing this earthly air. We have many children of all ages that are just wanting to be loved wanted and nurtured. Why not spend your energy on these children or are they not worth it?

**What if** you look at the mother and her values and beliefs?

Is it possible even a decent woman can make a mistake should she not be able to make an independent decision without our government holding her hand?

Is she no more allowed to choose abortion than the person who asks to not be resuscitated?

When talking about pain I cannot imagine the pain emotionally or physically that these children of Susan Smith, or Tina Lopez went through. Which one would be less painful? Abortion, or the children that died at the hands of their mothers? Who are we to decide for another woman, or person to have to raise a child for eighteen year if she, or they don't want to?

## Trimming the fat

With every president there seems to be a First Lady, each wanting to make a statement, or be remembered in some way or another. Our current First Lady Michelle Obama, who seems almost as mysterious as her husband. A woman who wants to make a difference. A woman that only after her husband became president, stated it was only then she became a proud American, really? Will she still be a proud American once her husband's term is up?

Michelle Obama is all about eliminating certain foods and snacks out of the schools. Is this an area that has been thoroughly studied? What is the reason for eliminating certain foods from the schools menus? If it is just to prevent obesity in the schools, would this not be an area that should be left to the parents and their own physicians? Is not our government infringing on our rights when they tell our children, what they can, or cannot eat, just simply for the purpose of shaping our children to something more presentable in their eyes?

Have they looked at how the children responded to the new menus? Are they concerned with the kids that won't eat the foods because they do not like it?

**What if** they do not eat because they are picky eaters?

**What if** they are hungry because they chose not to eat. Now you have students that are hungry and not focused on school work, but rather food.

**What if** we tell Michelle Obama she can't eat ice cream. We wouldn't want her to lose her girly figure. What's the difference with her figure and the children's?
What type of message is being sent to the children that are genetically obese? Is not there a different set of nutritional standards that are set for each child depending on their weight, age, metabolism, and their own family genetics?

**What if** we leave the nutrition to the parents? Is this really not the government censoring what we feed our children, pushing their morals and values upon us? Who are they to tell us how to raise our children, or is this a trade off for us telling them how to work?

Michelle Obama stated this is not her that is driving the nutritional battle forward but all of us?

**What if** we look at all the schools and what those trays look like?

**What if** we made kids get outside and play instead of having them work their fingers playing video games?

**What if** they had to do chores and other added responsibilities that kids now days just take for grant it, hoping someone else will do?

**What if** the government focused on those that are on welfare and other State aids? Maybe they could limit them, to nutritional foods and eliminate their snacks? Maybe it is those people who we need to focus on after all they appear to be eating ok, just no motivation to work.

## **Poor timing or poor judgment?**

Newlywed Army Captains Natalie and Edward Mallue were scheduled to get married at the Kaneohe Klipper Golf Course. They had sent an invitation to President Obama who sent them a letter respectfully declining. Yet president Obama seems to make it there on their scheduled wedding date?

Did he not really send them a letter signed by him? Did he not honestly know? The golf course chose to put a couple's wedding on hold for the President. Even if the golf course told their customers that all plans are subject to change, shouldn't they have brought this up to the President? Should it have not been his decision on kicking them off, after all he is their commander and chief? The couple seemed to be ok with the whole situation and seemed very honored on the President calling them.

It was their wedding day and if they are happy with
how it turned out, so am I
You can't say that the president doesn't make the news
even if it seems like lately his battles are with a club in
his hand on the green, or on vacation.

**What** if there were no golf courses out there, what
sport do you think the president would be into?

**Since he's good at bowing I might have to say
croquet.**

Remember The President of the United States represents
us Americans Let no other flag fly higher.

**What image do we Americans, want to portray?**

# CHAPTER THREE

## <u>Conceal or Smoke</u>

Colorado was the first State to legalize recreational
marijuana. Now the State voters are considering a ballot
for pot smokers to carry concealed firearms. The
Colorado Campaign for Equal Gun Rights is working
hard to get the 2016 ballot changed ignoring the guide
lines of the U.S. Bureau of Alcohol, Tobacco, Firearms.
The measure would change state law preventing
sheriffs from denying concealed carry permits because
of marijuana use.

Here we again have two sides that have strong
arguments. On the side of those that say it is their right
to carry concealed, that they are responsible and the
government should not try to impede, hinder or delay
what is already their right to carry. They are afraid that
if you put limitations on their rights to carry conceal,
that it may open doors for the government to try other
avenues and forms of restriction. This is a very
legitimate complaint.

On the other side you have those that believe if you can't carry in a bar or drink and carry that you shouldn't be able to with marijuana. They believe that marijuana will delay or disrupt your good judgment.

What is the purpose for smoking marijuana in the first place? Does it wake you up or make you more relaxed? Have they done tests on this to see the differences, whether or not there are differences?

I think truthfully and this is just my opinion on this particular subject. I have got a solution that could make everyone happy. If you leave it where there are no restrictions you make the gun owners happy, however it does come with consequences. If you are a gun owner and you get into an altercation where you have to pull and shoot, you have to understand you will come under scrutiny. When you are in court you will have to prove why you felt threatened or drew your gun to save another. Do you honestly think the prosecuting attorney or the victims lawyer won't challenge this area and more than likely win?

**What if** we let our law abiding American citizens make some sound decisions on their own.

**What if** we hold each person accountable  for their own actions?

**What if** we have those that want to smoke and shoot take a training seminar showing the differences just using training bullets. Would this not educate those that may honestly believe otherwise?

**Is not training more effective then restrictions, where people choose to defy our government?**

## Student loans or slavery

A student loan is a loan that is given for the purpose of helping a student financially. It is there to assist the student so they may stay focused on their studies. It is also there to encourage others to apply and register as well.
A student loan is only temporary, it is to be paid back at the completion of their schooling. Each student is responsible for his or her loans that they have accumulated.

The average cost for a student in a public college per year was around sixteen thousand dollars in State, out of State could be eighteen thousand on up. This is according to a census that was done in two thousand and ten, five years ago. Today the cost is closer to thirty or forty thousand a year. The cost all depend on the States themselves.

Let's look at a student that goes to college for four years at twenty thousand dollars a year, upon completion of his schooling he will walk out of the school owing a mere eighty thousand dollars. Is he guaranteed a job? Will he be able to pay this debt off in a reasonable amount of time?

**What if** the schools stopped exploiting our children who are only wanting to better themselves.

**What if** they came up with a formula that was more reasonable?

**What if** the student paid back their student loan in a percentage formula?
If we take a few minutes and look at this closer it might make better sense.

Say you go to school to be a police officer. Say they make fifty thousand dollars a year under this formula the students would have to pay twenty percent of their annual salary for schooling. Can we not educate our children without the teachers robbing them. If they were a Doctor that was making five hundred thousand dollars a year hypothetically He would have four years to pay back one hundred thousand dollars. If he were the police officer he would have four years to payback ten thousand dollars.

**What if** we tried making the student loans cheaper so that the students can graduate without being so much in debt?

 **What if** the college loan was only for twenty percent of one year's salary? This makes it cheaper more obtainable and depending on the career you choose, depended on what you paid. This way even though all loans would be different according to your studies they would all get paid off in a four year process, leaving all students debt free to get on their feet.

**What if** we ask the banks and the colleges for leniency when it came to educating our youth of tomorrow?

**What if** we had communities that went out of their way to push students to not only graduate, but to see they were placed back into our communities to help our communities grow and prosper.

**What if** we make sure that student loans were only for legalized citizens.

**What if** the colleges are looking at this the same way banks look at credit card holders, a long term debt that they control.
Maybe those in our society prefer others to suffer and struggle so as to make their lives more plush and comforting.

**What if** we look at education itself. A person with actual hands on experience compared to a person with a degree. Who would you want if you were a correctional officer and it is your first day on the job. Do you want the officer with years of experience or the one that's got a degree in criminal justice, who has never confronted a two hundred and thirty pound inmate that benches over four hundred pounds and is a high ranking gang member?

**What if** we look at work ethics just as much as we do education. The last example shows why having a degree is not always the best choice, or only choice. A good business uses both those with degrees and those with work experience.

As long as the young adults that are willing to get out there and work instead of going through college don't get punished.

**What if** we worked on building our youth of tomorrow showing respect of both our college graduates and hard working youth in the work force.

## <u>Finding a President</u>
Election time brings out politicians like Black Friday brings out the deal shoppers. That brings me to my next topic, women in the presidency.

I know the feminist will be ready to wage war on anyone, or group that challenges or brings up this issue of a female president.

Who are the feminist and what is feminism? The advocacy of women's rights on the grounds of political, social, and economic equality to men. I guess to be fare we need to look at the qualifications to be president. If we look at this area with open minded views we should be able to see clearly whether or not this is an option worth venturing into.

### Age and Citizenship requirements - US Constitution, Article II, Section 1

No person except a **natural born citizen**, or a citizen of the United States, at the time of the adoption of this Constitution, shall be eligible to the office of President; neither shall any person be eligible to that office who shall not have attained to the age of thirty-five years, and been fourteen years a resident within the United States.

### Term limit amendment - US Constitution, Amendment XXII, Section 1 - ratified February 27, 1951

No person shall be elected to the office of the President more than twice, and no person who has held the office of President, or acted as President, for more than two years of a term to which some other person was elected

President shall be elected to the office of the President more than once.

The President of the United States is the commander and chief he is the general of all generals. Do you think as president that he should have knowledge of how our military works?

**What if** we have a president that has no knowledge of the military?

**What if** we don't focus on whether the president is female but rather someone with a military background? We all know that Hillary Clinton is going to be running for that office most likely.

**What if** we look at how she did in the Benghazi crisis? Did she take ownership for the deaths of four Americans? Does she have a military background? Has she ever wore a uniform of any one of our military branches?

**What if** we look at this in another way. Say she is a coach of a football team. How can she coach if she don't have the skills to know what the players are doing right or wrong, cause she's never played?

**What if** we look at the term limits, according to the term limits no president can serve more than two terms.

**What if** she gets in office, is not her husband who is an ex-president going to have knowledge, access, and opportunity to put his influence in play? Is this not manipulation at its highest form? Could Bill and Hillary be the new age Bonnie and Clyde?

**What if** we look at why our politicians are constantly changing rules, views and opinions, to accommodate themselves.

**I stand by what I say, not what I said.**

## Red White and Blue

Sometimes issues are brought up unintentionally, for example the freedom of speech. We all know we have the right to speak whatever is on our mind, so long as it does not cause panic, or tarnish ones reputation.
 What about using the flag to speak? If you want to hold the flag as you take pride in being an American great, but for those that wish to light our flag on fire to burn and make a statement, think again.

We should show respect to our flag that has provided us with so many benefits. We can choose where we want to work, or where we want to live. We can decide on what we want to watch on TV. Sometimes I believe that protesters mean well as they rally for a cause, but to the soldier who's fighting over seas or that are just stationed overseas, they may see things differently. They may see you as someone who wishes to harm our country, mutiny, treason, and terrorism come to mind.

**What if** we look at those that burn our flag as a hate crime?

**What if** we went back to teaching our culture on the proper way to salute our flag, or fold it when taking it down?

**What if** we started flying our flags daily just because we are proud to be Americans?

**What if** we started saying the pledge of allegiance in the schools again? We have a right to free speech but speak as though you really want to be heard. Let the flag that guarded you and your freedom, be what you watch over, when you're so freely expressing yourself.

## **Register for life**

We finally have those that are convicted sex offenders, having to register as such in our communities. I think this is a great thing, anytime you can know in advance where a sexual predator is, it's to our advantage.

Knowing this when you send your children outside that there could be one or two in your immediate location, might make you think twice.

**What if** we look at whether or not sexual assaults have gone down or up with those that have registered?

**What if** we look at has it been easier to track them since they have had to register?

**What if** we look at doing drug dealers, murderers in the same manner?
Why not seriously think about this? We only have a certain amount of children per family. I know I want to do everything I can to prevent my children from being harmed, whether by a child molester, or a drug dealer. To me there is no difference both will cause harm physically and mentally. We should love our children enough to prevent them from any type of harm.

**What if** the next time you take your children out trick or treating and you tell them not this house because this is where a sexual predator lives, or a drug dealer. To end this I just need to ask you, is any of this registering?

## The most dangerous monster of all, is the one that's invisible.

## <u>Federally funded food stamps</u>

Has any of you been on food stamps? I know there is nothing wrong with this. I have been on them before, when I was between jobs while I was out looking for another job. I think it is a great program for those that use it for what it is intended for, a short term financial aid to assist you while you get back on your feet.
The problem is when you see the same people on it year after year, with no job in between. Let us look at the requirements.

## Financial Requirements

Qualifying for Illinois SNAP benefits is mainly determined by a family's combined gross monthly income, any resources in the home, the household's combined monthly expenses, and the number of people eating together in the home.

If any household member is over age 60 or disabled or you have a larger family, the higher the allowable monthly income. If unsure about your family's financial eligibility, check the SNAP eligibility calculator, available online at: www.michigan.gov/documents. It provides a quick and easy screener for the program.

A family may meet all the income requirements but not qualify for food stamps in the state of Illinois. Individuals on strike or capable of working but not actively seeking employment are not to be approved to receive SNAP benefits. In addition, some immigrants, boarders and residents of various institutions may not qualify for food stamps.

Families who receive money for groceries through Illinois's SNAP program have to meet certain income requirements. Maximum income levels depends on household sizes as listed on next page.

## Household Size Monthly Income

| | |
|---|---|
| 1 | $1,174 |
| 2 | $1,579 |
| 3 | $1,984 |
| 4 | $2,389 |
| 5 | $2,794 |
| 6 | $3,200 |
| 7 | $3,605 |
| 8 | $4,010 |
| 9 | $4,416 |

In households with more than ten people, add $406 per person to calculate the maximum monthly income allowable.

**What if** we actually have someone monitor these people and make sure they are truly seeking employment.

**What if** those people that get caught feeding hamburger to their dogs, or milk to their cats get charged with fraud.

I'm not talking at looking at the ones that are on it a year or less but those over a year. My entire life I have never gone more than six months without a job, more like three months to be accurate.

**What if** we look at those that apply for State aid also must apply for jobs at the same time?

## **Sledding a thing of the past**

They talked about banning sledding in Dubuque, Iowa and a few other cities. Yep, I was thinking the same thing. Are we still in the same book? Unfortunately we are. Why would someone write about sledding in a book about <u>Changing America with What " if's"?</u> I guess it is because there are people out there that won't stop trying to take from you and I. Now they are out there trying to band sledding in Dubuque, Iowa. I had to see this on the news to believe it for myself.

How ridiculous and absurd. If they band sledding, they will then move to skiing this could affect the winter Olympics dramatically, yes I'm being sarcastic, but truthfully what's next amusement parks, golfing, swimming?

Who are these people who put these laws, bands, and restrictions on all of us? Have none of these people ever went sledding before? Our rights are being chipped away by idiocracy, lunacy and just plain ignorance.

It really comes down to money and accountability. The city of Dubuque, Iowa is not wanting to be sued for someone else's mistake. Remember the saying it just takes one to screw it up for the rest of us. That is exactly what is happening, someone got hurt having fun so now they want to have someone pay for their mistake.

**What if** we tell them no.

**What if** we stop giving in to these people that just expect hand outs for every little thing that doesn't go their way? These people in charge should be strong enough to stand for the rest of us, who are the ones who elected them in to office in the first place.

**What if** we look at what twenty years might look like from now. You serious dad, when you were young you went outside without a helmet and knee pads? Weren't you scared? You said you went sledding, what is that dad? What is skiing? You think I could take a bath without my floaters? No son there is a law where you have to keep your floaters on.

I know it sounds farfetched but is it really? Only time will tell how much change will take place?

**What if** you turn the page in this book and think of this book as just entertainment and not as a book of **What "If's"**.

I hope that as Americans we can stay strong and united, for it will take all of us to change the few, who only have their own interests in mind. I understand that there may be some areas where sledding can and could be dangerous, but to band a whole community out of financial fear is ridiculous.

Maybe we need to take our sleds to Capitol Hill and slide down the steps to show them what type of fun they are taking away from our American children. Here we have a sport you actually have to work at in order to have fun, once you slide down you have to walk your way back to the top.

## **Blue funeral**

The New York police officers once again show unity as they turn their backs on Mayor De-Blassio as he speaks at the funeral of officer Wenjian Liu. Mayor De-Blassio stated the officers who turned their backs on him only showed disrespect to officer Wenjian Liu and his family and those that were there to honor him.

I think if we truly look at this, those that turned their backs on the Mayor, were not doing it out of disrespect to officer Wenjian Liu, but instead trying to speak out in his behalf.

**What if** Mayor De-Blassio would not have provoked the poor communities by encouraging them it was ok to harm a police officer?

**What if** Mayor De-Blassio could take back all his statements that not only falsely accused an entire police force of being reckless and ruthless, but did cause officer Wenjian Liu to leave this place before his time was truly up. Where is the respect to his family who will never be able to talk to him, or hug him ever again?

When it comes time for voting again, I'm sure there will be a lot that will check the respect box by Mayor De-Blassio on the ballot.

## While the man in the tie, continues to lie

## Let our families in blue continue on true

### Bible banning

A twelve year old boy from Missouri, who was going to Bueker Middle School in Marshall, was told to put his book away it wasn't permitted in the classroom. The boy was reading the Bible to himself. This is a clear violation of both the boys freedom to religion and his freedom of speech.

 I am no lawyer, it is still just my opinion, but seriously is this not a perfect example of censorship?

I would think in a school, that they would be the last to want to start censoring.

**What if** we buck up to all the Bucker Middle Schools and let them know we are not going to bow down to tyranny. We have rights, as do our children.

Are we not supporting the atheist in schools by not allowing our children their right to even silently open the book of their choice?

I can think of many more books, that are far less worthy to be opened. When you watch shows on the Bible most the time they are on the channels like Discovery, or the History channel.

**What if** the Bible was talked about in school, if nothing else under history? If we can't talk about it in history class, what about Science with evolution and the beginning of the world. Maybe we need to just have our parents teach us about how the schools fear retribution and being sued just by talking about God.

## To teach some things and not  everything is injustice, as well as falsely.

Do we not teach about slavery in schools? It is something many are not proud of, but it is history and it shouldn't be forgotten. What is the reason America even exist today? What was our reason for venturing in the direction of the new world?

To be a pastor you have to study on all the different religions and events. So by censoring this topic are we also not violating the right of a child who may one day wish that he knew more in school on the bible so that he could make an educated choice on following his career dream?

Teaching now days censorship, is like buying a car without seeing any numbers. It just does not make sense. It is not even ethically or morally correct. Let me end this on a moment of silence, Amen.

## <u>News Alert, twelve killed in Parris</u>

Twelve citizens killed in Parris, France. Three gunman still on the loose. They have been described as Muslim yet the president never addressed them as Muslim terrorist, why?

When will we see our enemy for who they are? It is not like a wolf hiding in sheep's clothing. What if this again is a stalling technique used by the President to minimize the damage of the Muslim-hood? I wonder how long till the President will scamper on to vacation again? As long as he isn't planning on going sledding in Dubuque, Iowa he will be fine.

## Call the terrorist what they are killers.

When the President spoke, he spoke from the Oval office. But he appeared soft spoken and beaten. His eyes didn't match his words. He looked like just a normal man who was talking with a cup of coffee in his hand. He didn't present himself as a football player ready for the next play, but rather as a fan watching from the sidelines. Wow sounds like I heard him talk like this before. Mr. President we need you to take charge and get us some results.

# **Vindictive Veto's**

The president has already stated he was going to veto the republicans. If he can't have everything his way he is going to be that kid who took his ball home just because he couldn't be in charge.

The president has the right to veto, but it should be used with caution and diligence. The White House is not a gym where you go and play games, it is a place of work where those that have been elected to work there, work for us. I think it is funny how many seem to forget this.

**What if** we the people had the right to veto?

**What if** we stopped focusing on republicans and democrats and started focusing on Americans, after all it is the Americans that run this country.

**What if** we challenged the veto with the check and balance system that is and has been in place for decades? Hum, **what if**.

**What if** the President came out telling us of his decisions in detail and why he will or will not do something so the American people can know what decisions are being made, how they are being made and whether their interests are being well served. These are his words from earlier if you remember.

# Life or Death sentence

This is an area that gets debated at times, mostly after something tragic has happened. We get riled when our children and parents get hurt, maimed, or killed. We look to law enforcement to apprehend the criminals that do us harm.

What we have no control of, is the courts that give all those of guilt and innocence a fare shot to freedom. It is better to let ten guilty walk then it is to make one innocent do time. This is one of the arguments with getting rid of the death sentence, because **what if** we put to death one that could be proven later as innocent. If we prove he was innocent but now he is dead we lose what our intended goal always was, to set an innocent man free.

Some think it is inhumane to kill, whether it be by hanging, electricity, lethal injections, or a firing squad. I'm sure there really isn't anyway that dying can look or feel great. It is what it is. Those that received the death sentence had to have gone in front of a judge or jury, hopefully their cases were heard impartially giving them every opportunity to argue their cases.

Whether you believe or don't believe, we have to trust our courts to see that a fare and impartial trial is and was conducted and hope that those that are sentenced to death truly are guilty of what their sentence is.

Let us hope we don't later say **what if** we forgot something or cover up evidence in a manner that is deceitful. On the other side you have those that feel a life sentence is to good for the one convicted of a heinous crime. They do not like knowing that they will get three square meals a day, cable TV, medical attention and another day of life. They see also that we the tax payers are the ones that inevitably foot the bill. I see both sides and understand their reasoning.

**What if** we had more death penalties followed through with? Would the criminals think twice then?

**What if** we took their TV's and radios? Would they hate prison more? I can only say that whether you like it or not if you give them nothing you will turn even the petty criminal into a killer who becomes vengeful of his own treatment feeling, he is the victim. This then puts all our law abiding officers and staff at risk. Some see a prison as a punishment, where prisoners are to be punished. Others see prison as a educational opportunity to teach and re-educate them back in to society as law abiding citizens. The truth is prison is about maintaining custody and control. It is keeping the inmate in a guarded facility until their time is up, at which then hopefully they will have learned their lesson.

**What if** we look at how many convicted felons finish out their time and never commit again?

**Whether life or death it is still time away from society.**

# Pledge of Allegiance

I pledge allegiance to the flag
If you can't say that you must be vague
They took the allegiance out of the schools
If you ask me I think their fools


They said there were conflicts of religion
That's like comparing an eagle to a pigeon
The only religion said is one nation under God
Where are these people living under the sod


The pledge of allegiance is pride to our service
But say it in school and watch them get nervous
The allegiance in schools will never be repeated
All because someone wanted to stay seated


The pledge of allegiance was our country's pride
Now it's hardly known nationwide
It's up to us to let our children know
It's pride in our country that will help them grow

## UNITED STATES SUPREME COURT BUILDING

# "WHAT IF"

## WE SOUGHT JUSTICE AT ITS HIGHEST DESTINATION?

# CHAPTER FOUR

## <u>Presidential denial</u>

Why is it that president Obama seems to shy away from world events, especially with Muslim controversies? If we look at president Obama from the beginning, we see a president that talks about transparency. As our commander and chief he has continued to defy showing his birth certificate. He has changed his religious status from christen to Muslim, back and forth like he were playing Three Ball Monty with all of us.

The speech he gave on Jim Foley beheading, only reassured many Americans, that president Obama lacked sincerity by going right out afterwards playing golf, laughing, joking and having a good time.

I have not even heard him speak about the terrorist in Parris, France as Muslim extremist. What is it that the word Muslim ceases to exist in times of turmoil with him?

**Muslim if you can't say it, you can't address it.**

**What if** when he mentioned transparency he just meant us being transparent so he would know everything we are doing? A great dictator knows all that goes on around them and trusts no one.

**What if** President Obama was one of them? What better way to attack America, than from inside the White House. Our symbol of power, freedom and democracy.

**What if** president Obama just wants to be known as a peace President? A President who did everything to avoid war.

Any and all **what if** questions brought up in regards to the President should at least be looked at even with a short glimpse. He is our President that we elected to represent us. Why should we not look at him closely, it's nothing personal. I'm sure he as President and as a professional would not be offended, unless he had something to hide.

We all are able to be drug tested, at our places of employment. Should we be offended, thinking they don't trust us?

We get audited by the I.R.S. parents do interviews on people that they want to leave their children with before they make their final decisions. We have back ground checks run on people before they get hired at certain jobs.

In some State jobs the employees have to take an annual ethics test, Though the hire up you go the less the word ethics appears on applications, or in the work environment. Why is that?

**What if** we push our leaders to higher standards that equal their higher pay and more power over us? President Obama we're waiting, just say Muslim extremist I know you can do it. Hold them accountable as if they were a Christians.

Let's look at Muslim terror attacks closer. The following is a list of Islamic terrorist attacks that have received significant press coverage since 1980.

**April 18, 1983** – The U.S. Embassy bombing, Beirut, Lebanon by the Islamic Jihad Organization. 63 dead, 120 injured.

**July 7, 1989** – Tel Aviv Jerusalem bus 405 suicide attack, near Kiryat Yearim. 16 dead

**March 12, 1993** – Serial blasts in Mumbai kill 257 people.

**December 24, 1994** – Air France Flight 8969 hijacking in Algiers by 3 members of Armed Islamic Group of Algeria. 7 killed including 4 hijackers.

**June 25, 1996** – Khobar Towers bombing, 20 killed, 372 wounded.

**November 17, 1997** – Luxor massacre, 6 armed Islamic terrorists attacked tourists at the Luxor ruins. 62 killed, 26 injured.

**February 14, 1998** – A total of 58 people were killed and over 200 injured in 12 bomb attacks in 11 places, in the city of Coimbatore, Tamil Nadu.

**August 7, 1998** – United States embassy bombings in Tanzania and Kenya. 224 dead, 4000+ injured

<u>Let us look at only the American attacks since 2000 and then see if we are just over reacting</u>

**October 12, 2000** – Attack on the USS Cole in the Yemeni port of Aden. 17 American sailors were killed, 39 injured.

**September 11, 2001** – 4 planes hijacked by 19 al-Qaeda hijackers: two planes crashed into World Trade Center and one into the Pentagon. Nearly 3000 dead.

**June 1, 2009** - Little Rock recruiting office shooting by Abdulhakim Muhajid Muhammad. 1 killed and 1 injured.

**November 5, 2009** – Fort Hood shooting, at Fort Hood near Killeen, Texas. 13 dead, 33 injured.

**May 1, 2010** – Times Square car bombing attempt, New York, New York, USA. Faisal Shahzad, an Islamic Pakistani American who received an American citizenship in December 2009, attempted to detonate a car bomb in Times Square working with the Pakistani Taliban or Tehrik-I-Taliban Pakistan.

**September 11, 2012** – Benghazi attack on the U.S. Consulate. 4 dead, 11 injured.

**April 15, 2013** – Boston Marathon bombings. Two brothers, Tamerlan and Dzhokhar Tsarnev, planted two bombs near the finish line of the Boston Marathon.

**October 23, 2014** – Zale H. Thomson, also known as Zaim Farouq Abdul-Malik, attacked four New York policemen in the subway with a hatchet, severely injuring one in the back of the head and injuring another policeman in the arm before being shot to death by the remaining officers, who also shot a bystander killed 3 and injured 183 others.

When our leaders stop denying what's really going on, then maybe we can get back to being Americans and destroy, eliminate, exterminate whatever you wish to call it. Let's just Protect America.

# 911

## A day that will never be forgotten

To every American that was innocently traveling that day not knowing they were in harm's way till it was too late. To every American that witnessed this barbaric act of pure hatred. To every American that lost someone close to them. To every American that saw their country attacked.

We will rise to any occasion, we always have and our enemies know this. To all those who have suffered I am sorry for your losses, but those that died will forever be seen as heroes.

# Missing in Action

I think our president has gone missing in action. I would lock down all golf courses and vacation spots until he was found. What is our president trying to tell France and our other allies? Is he trying to tell them he is scared? Maybe he is trying to tell them he don't care. Maybe he is trying to say I am Muslim and am not going to offend my people, no not the American my people, the Muslim my brothers people.

**What if** we impeached the president on the grounds of being un-American?

**What if** we put someone in the presidency that was going to be transparent? France stood strong and united waving their red white and blue flag in a rally against Radical Islamic. Once again President Obama looked weak not showing up, or sending anyone to represent our country.

**What if** our country was being represented?

**What if** we are representing the meek and indecisive?

There is only one reason I can think of for our president not to show and it is to once again divide our great nation from our allies. We are either with them or against them. He appears to be trying to divide us from within our own country by race.

He has been more forgiving to the Radical Muslims, just look how he words everything careful not to offend them, or his own people.

Remember to debate any of this is to have an argument on both sides. Well do we have an argument?

In our country he divides us by race, encouraging distrust among whites and blacks.

In our country and abroad he divides our religion, by banning Christianity while silently supporting the Muslim nations.

In the world he divides our country from our allies, by showing no unity  in a time of crisis where unity matters and our allies rely on our support.

## **Five score years ago**

Five days from now we will be celebrating Martin Luther King Jr. day. Why is this day so important and who is Martin Luther King Jr.? What is this dream that everyone talks about in regards to Martin Luther King Jr.? Well August 28,1963 "<u>I Have a Dream</u>" is a public speech delivered by American civil rights activist Martin Luther King, Jr. on August 28, 1963, in which he calls for an end to racism in the United States.

Delivered to over 250,000 civil rights supporters from the steps of the Lincoln Memorial during the March on Washington, the speech was a defining moment of the American Civil Rights Movement.

Martin Luther King Jr. was a great leader, he displayed that by how many followers he had and how peaceful he was able to demonstrate with a quarter of a million people by his side in a time where racism issues were still volatile.

Martin Luther King Jr. talked about the Emancipation Proclamation being a great beacon light of hope to millions of Negro slaves, who had been seared in the flames of withering injustice.

One hundred years later the Negro is still not free, crippled by the manacles of segregation and the chains of discrimination. He states one hundred years later the Negro lives on a lonely island of poverty One hundred years later the Negro is still languished in the corners of American society and finds himself in exile in his own land.

He stated that the signing of the Constitution and the Declaration of independence was a promissory note to which every American was to fall heir. That all men yes, black men as well as white men would be guaranteed the unalienable rights of life, liberty and a pursuit of happiness. He stated that America had defaulted on the promissory note as far as with the citizens of color.

They were gathered together to demand the riches of freedom and the security of justice. He reminded all that were there that this was not a time to take tranquilizing drug of gradualism. It was time to make real the promises of democracy.

He stated 1963 was not the end, but the beginning. He also stated "In the process of gaining our rightful place, we must not be guilty of wrongful deeds. Let us not seek to satisfy our thirst for freedom by drinking from the cup of bitterness and hatred.

**What if** Al Sharpton and Reverend Wright would heed the words of this great leader?

Martin Luther King Jr. stated."We must forever conduct our struggle on the high plane of dignity and discipline. We must not allow our creative protests to degenerate into physical violence.

**What if** those that had spoke out in Ferguson, Missouri would have only listened to these words spoken two and a half score ago by this great leader Martin Luther King Jr.

Martin Luther King Jr. stated. "We can never be satisfied as long as the Negro is the victim of the unspeakable horrors of police brutality.

**What if** we look just at that statement. Are we not any better off now than we were fifty years ago with police brutality? I think there are more whites now out there that are on the side of the black communities.

**What if** those that call themselves victims today are looked at closer. How many of them that yell police brutality are criminals or have been arrested, or charged with a crime?

How many yell police brutality just because they are being watched in a mall as they shop? How many that yell police brutality, do so from outside a heavily populated area where crime isn't rampant?

Martin Luther King Jr. stated " We can never be satisfied as long as the Negro's basic mobility is from a smaller ghetto to a larger one. We can never be satisfied as long as our children are stripped of their adulthood and robbed of their dignity by signs stating "For whites only". I agree with him on this, but **what if** we look at the ghettos as a place to start.

**What if** we turn the ghettos in to nice living communities for those that wish to live a crime free life, safe from murderers and rapists, where no gangs may harbor or infest the communities that have so long struggled. Where the children will no longer be robbed of their adult lives, but their childhood as well.

I have a dream that one day all will be treated as individuals that are responsible for their own actions. Where race and sexual origin will no longer play a role in how we will, or think we should be treated. Where you get things by earning them where one hand will hold another not by color, but by Americanism..

## **Terrorist on the loose**

The American nurse Kaci Hickox  from Maine went to West Africa to treat Ebola. She went as an American and as a nurse to save lives. She was an American hero. She went to put her life on the line for others who were not American and were less fortunate. When she stepped off the plane she was in a fight with a deadly disease. She was a hero because she was willing to sacrifice her life to help others.

She then returned to the States, though this time when she got off the plane she was again in a fight not just with Ebola, but her own morals and values. Kaci Hickox suddenly rebelled and defied the quarantine order that was in place. She stated she was in negotiations to end this amicably. The State was wanting her to stay in quarantine another twelve days. The locals were outraged at her arrogant stance on the whole issue.

Why would a nurse who is willing to sacrifice herself to help those that are not American, then come back and put everyone she knew, her family, her friends and every other person at risk just for her own selfish whims?

She had no problem helping those outside our country, but then sat thumbing her nose at the press or at you and I. Should she not be labeled a terrorist? What is the difference with her and a terrorist that stands in the middle of a crowd before he blows himself and many others up?

What's the difference with her and the Terrorist that flew our planes into the Twin Towers,  or the pentagon? I am sure those people on those planes would have liked the opportunity to have gotten off the planes first and those inside the Twin Towers would have liked enough notification to have left the building before their lives were forever taken just because of a cause, or a belief.

**What if** we look at what she was. She was a nurse a person professionally trained to care for the sick or infirm. Why did she go to West Africa in the first place? I believe that she went to go help the ill, so why would she then come home and complain about having to stay in the comforts of her own home for a designated amount of time to ensure that every man, woman and child was safe.

**What if** she doesn't value Americans? Why else would she want to risk our lives so she could go enjoy a moment of fresh air on a bicycle?

**What if** she is trying to tell us that Doctors and nurses are above morality.

**What if** she went to jail for attempted murder, at the very least loose her credentials to serve in the medical field as she has shown us her ethical standards are far below the type of medical standards I or my family would deem necessary to treat us.

Just because no one contracted the disease from her doesn't make her any less guilty. A man who pulls the trigger of a gun at someone but it misfires does that not still make it attempted murder? She said she was in negotiations to end this amicably, which is another way of saying friendly. She is in no way a friend and in no way a professional. She chose her morality over all of us. If nothing else we could show her our appreciations by giving her a one way ticket for life to West Africa, to me she has picked her new home.

I fought for my country and I took an oath to protect my country from foreign and domestic atrocities.

**What if** America stood up to all these who wish to harm America for their own causes?

## America we've come to take you back

## <u>Lost Innocents</u>

On a Saturday afternoon in Maryland one mile from where Danielle and Alexander Meitiv live their two children ages ten and six were walking home from the Silver Spring park on Georgia Avenue.

Danielle and Alexander were aware of their children's walk home. It was seen as a chance for their children to show some independence, but the local authorities seen it otherwise. The Department of Human services is now investigating the matter saying it was neglectful.

Ok now I am waiting to hear what really happened. I guess I missed something? What, are you serious, I didn't miss anything?

They are calling the children walking home by themselves, neglect? I walked to and from school on many occasions with my brothers who were just a year or two apart from me. We were not much different in age then those kids. We went trick or treating without our parents at ten years old in the dark. Wow talk about opportunity for the predator.

I was watching a female legal consultant. She was on Fox News as she talked about the Meitiv parents. She stated that they were lazy and neglectful and implying they were irresponsible. Who is she to defame the character of these two people? Is she stating this all because of this one incident, or does she have more incidents?

She stated save the free range for the chickens. I'm sure she was just being sarcastic, otherwise she may be investigated by PETA later on. When will enough be enough? When my kids tell me dad I am not doing the dishes, there are some that are glass I might break one. It could happen.

This woman talked about they could have been killed or robbed. They could have froze to death or had heat exhaustion as well. There are a lot of scenarios out there but what if we look on the other side.

How about those young children that call 911 when there is an emergency, or go next door unsupervised to get assistance? What about those children that notice a stranger in their neighborhood. Who do you think taught these kids these things? What about teachers teaching kids the saying Stranger danger? Why do they need to learn this if the parents are going to be right there? What if we then make all kids learn to ride a bicycle with training wheels, when you think your child is ready to ride without them you notify Department of Human Services.

Let us wake up and remember the old days. **What if** we let our parents be parents and make decisions? For those could haves and would haves, if you are so worried about the predators out there arrest them. Why should our children have to be punished for those that could and will commit offenses.

Stop releasing them once they get sentenced. The woman stated the children were better off with Foster care than the parents the kids have now. When she was challenged on the kids that get abused in the Foster care, she was quick to say we can't judge them all. So why is she judging this couple with their children She is judging their entire parenting skills. I grew up with kids of all ages and many were in school with me, yet we all had different curfews and times to eat. We all went to a variety of churches and had different activities we did while at home. We were all parented differently.

I remember my parents telling me when I stated well Joeys mom lets him do that. They would say You're not Joey and we are not his parents.

To end this let's just say parenting is not always easy but it is the parents that made us all who we are today and yes I am talking to us adults.


## Sniper assault

Michael Moore, Michael Moore, who is Michael Moore? Well he is an American who wishes to express how he was raised and express the values he was taught to believe in.

His dad was in the First Marine Division in the South Pacific in World War II. His father's brother, his uncle, Lawrence Moore, was an Army paratrooper and was killed by a Japanese sniper 70 years ago next month according to Michael Moore. He stated his dad said that Snipers were cowards, that they don't believe in fighting fare. That only a coward shoots someone who can't shoot back.

Well let me first show my respect to Michael Moore's family who did serve in a time of war, or peace. I'm not sure if Michael Moore had ever served in the military, because War is no game people are going to die. I am not afraid to say I will do anything I have to, to save myself and to get home to my family. Michael Moore is quick to call these snipers cowards, Does he even know what it takes to just become a sniper let alone after you graduate and get put in special details where you are really on your own.

I understand him being loyal to his father who's brother was killed by a sniper. It would only be natural to say and feel the way he does, but if you pull back and look at war. Does he think the pilots of bombers who take out even more while not knowing their targets specifically? What about the artillery are they again not the same cowards? Then you have chemical war fare. Here more cowards releasing poisons out in the atmosphere. What about when a platoon is over run by a company?

Wow the more I think about this the more I think war is not fare.

**What if** we ask Michael Moore what would be a fare way to fight. Truth is, it will never be fare, it's war and as sad as it is people will die, it is up to us to see our service men and women come home. If we were playing cowboys and Indians, or cops and robbers we could do fare, or do over's. I was stationed in 2nd Bn. 9th Marines STA. PLT. I know what it is like to wear the uniform of our American Soldiers. The hardest thing is fighting for our country knowing we have people who wish to protest and know nothing about how the military operates.

I would like to say I in no way wish to purposely insult Michael Moore, but rather only try and understand his way of thinking. He does have a right to his opinion and even if I do not agree with it doesn't mean he shouldn't be able to express it, after all his father and uncle both served and if nothing else out of respect for them.

I hope that you are proud of our service members for fighting for your freedoms.

**What if** you at least think about how you make war fare and share it with everyone. Maybe we need someone to think outside the box.

**What if** his uncle were alive today, I'm sure he would be proud of Michael for wanting to stay so loyal. He may though have a completely different outlook on the sniper than his brother though.

I understand he is not here and he may or may not agree with his brother and nephew, but how does Michael Moore think he was able to come to this country if not at some point by bloodshed.

I really don't think he is a bad guy, I think he is just misguided in the reality of war. Until you have seen casualties on the field and understand both sides of the battlefield you will never truly understand.

One more question, what do you think of the politicians who send us over to war while they stay out of harm's way?

# Stay Focused

**Sniper, one shot one kill**
**Taking out one, to save the many.**

# CHAPTER FIVE

## <u>Remembering Rosa Parks</u>

Today we are celebrating the day of Martin Luther King Jr., but I think we can celebrate Rosa Parks as well. She was a woman with true character.

On December 1, 1955, Rosa Parks, a 42-year-old African-American seamstress, refused to give up her seat to a white man. Rosa Parks lived in Montgomery, Alabama. In that city the first rows of seats were reserved for whites only; while African-Americans, who paid the same ten cent fare as the whites, were required to find seats in the back. If all the seats were taken but another white passenger boarded the bus, then a row of African-American passengers sitting in the middle of the bus would be required to give up their seats, even if it meant they would have to stand. while riding on a city bus.

I understand that this is a touchy subject, so why do we continue to talk about it? I think we are here to support America. We have to at times look back and say we were wrong and then learn from it and move on. Rosa Parks taught us that one person can make a difference.

We should not look back and forget our history. We should not look ahead and seek vengeance for what has happened in the past.

**What if** we try to see if what we did in the past was intentional out of hatred, or if ignorance played a part in it. We now celebrate Martin Luther King Day as a national holiday. Businesses shut down, there are no schools that day. There is black history month that is celebrated.

**What if** we had a White history month? Do you think we would offend anyone? I hear it all the time about how inmates in the prison system blame the whites for their misfortune, some of what they say I think is correct, but I think we need to look at solutions, not blame and justification.

Like I said earlier One person can make a difference, Rosa Parks did sixty years ago when she chose to take a stand. When will the next Rosa Parks take a stand and clean up the ghettos, take responsibility on and encourage an honest trade?

**What if** someone with credentials, or was well known and liked for example Oprah Winfrey helped push these communities to look out after each other and assist your neighbors. President Obama and the others we have talked about earlier have done nothing but justify why they are angry and act out. It was over half a century ago time to move on. I am ready to build America, let's not become paralyzed by the past. Growth only comes from being open and the willingness to change.

## History has proven to be what was, leaving our future to yet be proven.

## All Winners

Arroyo Valley High School basketball coach suspended after team wins (161-2) I guess there are a few areas we could look at here, let's start off with the team winning. I would like to know why they would suspend their coach who has apparently done a great job with Arroyo Valley Girls High School basketball team. Did he get suspended because the score was so over whelming?

**What if** he as a coach showed compassion for the other team by having his players slack off? This would be teaching them to win honorably.

**What if** instead of suspending the coach, we ask why did the other team loose so badly? Maybe that coach should be suspended?

**What if** we look at the school administrators that schedule the games, are you telling me the other team was even in the same league? I understand that the one team was playing far above their expectations, while the other team had been struggling all season?

**What if** we leave things as they are?

**What if** we pat the kids on the back who were so far behind and still didn't give up. They are true sportsman's who show persistence, unwavering determination and the ability to lose on their side of the ball with dignity as well.

 **What if** they continued to play because their coach had taught them perseverance? Now it sounds like we have nothing but winners all the way around. One Coach won with  a superior team, one coach won by showing his team could handle losing with their heads held high. One team won because They played hard. The other team one because they never gave up. In the end it is not the score that counts it is the acceptance that you do your best no matter what the odds are. It's not whether you win or lose, but how you play the game.

Suddenly they forget this? I was taught this from day one and it is still in practice today. I understand they may say that is why they suspended their coach. But then your focusing on the score not everyone out there giving it their best.

I think we insult the kids that lost by so much when you don't praise them for not giving up, but rather you focus on pitting them because of such a poor score. I just want to say they are all true champions in my book.

How many professional football and basketball players could learn from this game? I say give the coach his job back and fix this mistake that clearly wasn't thought through.

## **America Remembered**

American made, Born in the USA, Uncle Sam wants you, Amen, Red, White and blue, Praise the Lord, I pledge allegiance to the flag of the United States of America, American pride, United we stand divided we fall, freedom, Super Power. These are words we grew up with, or at least I did. Now I look at these words and see them differently.

American made seems to be a thing of the past, close to extinction as businesses make and take their products overseas taking away the ability for us Americans to grow and prosper. Born in the USA, again just a formality or technicality. Anyone can become president even a foreigner if he knows, or has the ability to stall for the years he's in office. All he or she has to do is not show their birth certificate. Red, white and blue use to be the symbolism for a strong America. I do not blame our country, I blame our leaders who do everything they can to have their cake and eat it too.

The other day it appeared the Red, White and Blue seemed stronger in France where they rallied strong in the masses to fight against radical Islamists, waving their flag standing united against those few who wish to oppress us all, one nation at a time.

That brings us to, Uncle Sam wants you. We do not see that much anymore. Maybe it is because when that came out we had more pride, stronger values. We had presidents that were not afraid to shake their fist at those who wish to trespass with our freedom.

**What if** we stop shutting down military bases and sending troops home before the war is over?

**What if** before we get into a war we actually have a plan A, if not a plan B?

**What if** we wave our flag again as Americans and stir up the radical Islamists making them expose themselves, let freedom ring once again. I would have a hard time letting my son fight for our country under president Obama who appears weak and anything but transparent. I pledge allegiance to the flag of the United States of America, that means you are taking an oath to your country to stand by her and protect her, to honor her, love her and care for her. Most people enjoy the fourth of July but do they even think about it being Independence Day? Most people focus on just drinking, cooking out and watching the fireworks on a warm summers night. I enjoy this all too, but let us not forget we are doing this, all because of the independence we earned by the Americans who fought for us back then.

Super Power though we may still be, under this presidency I think our Allies see us more as a pawn if nothing else a super power with handcuffs on. We need to show we are not the supply country we are the country.

Amen, praise the Lord, in God we trust, Do you swear to tell the truth so help you God? Yes our religion seems to be constantly tested by those in politics who have nothing better to do than to try and win extra votes. Let us not forget God he is the one that showed us how to get to this great land. He is the one who helped us fight for our freedom.

In the movie Heart Break Ridge Clint Eastwood played the Marine Gunnery Sergeant, who to me represented the people of this country and the Major was like the politicians who was out of touch with reality. He was in charge with no true knowledge or experience. It was his arrogance and apathy that Clint Eastwood had to fight against not for himself but for all of his soldiers. He still had not lost the morality of protecting those he would be leading into war. Through the movie he was challenged but never did he bow down, or give up on what he believed in.

**What if** we fought for what we believed in and stood united against those who lack the knowledge, wisdom, or courage? This book isn't about rebellion, it's about becoming united together all of us.

I remember my child hood days where life seemed so simple. Where my parents took care of everything. Americans would stand up and salute the flag or put their hands over their hearts out of respect to Old Glory. I do not care who steps in to this country as long as they love her, respect her and its people. Let those who wish to harm her have a one way ticket back in a coffin, that's if their people will pay us for the coffin of course.

## America's future depends on the What "if's"

## <u>Password Authority</u>

Illinois law allowing school Administrators to get pass words of their students social media if they feel there is a concern?

What does the school have to do with the students social life? Is this not a violation of their right to privacy? Should not the concern be brought to the parents and maybe local authorities and go through the courts and get a proper search warrant for a particular student, or specific reason each time an issue comes up? What justifies an issue? Who makes the final call?

**What if** this violates the parents rights to parent their own children?

**What if** a student wants to embarrass another student by falsely accusing them knowing other information may come out?

**What if** you find something, then what? Do you spank them, or ground them, do you expel, or suspend them from class, do you charge them with a crime, or do you go after their parents?

Who decides on the punishment The School Administrator, Law enforcement, Parents, who? How will the students view honesty, truthfulness, Who will they go to with their issues?

What separates a teacher from a parent? How would a math teacher be better suited to parent than the children's own parents, who hopefully is instilling their own set of values and beliefs into their own child continuing to help American families grow. Many kids don't have both parents, so are we not taking away the other parent by giving more authority to the schools?

## School's call it detention, parent's call it grounding. We know what the law calls it serving time.

Let us unite and support the families and be there for them. Let the parents come to the schools and ask for the assistance giving the parents the power to lead and raise their own children with our schools supporting them.
Parents are quite capable of utilizing their assets in a time of crisis. We call doctors, Lawyers, ministers, friends and relatives. If we do not believe in our parents, why should the children?

# **Five Terrorists released**

Five Taliban released from Guantanamo Bay detention center. The Obama administration has released five Guantanamo Bay prisoners after an administration task force determined they no longer posed a threat. Are we Americans ok with this? I thought President Obama stated he was going to be transparent, oh maybe he was talking translucent, where he would pick and choose what he wanted us to see in a blurred obscure way.

I think it just shows his lack of knowledge when it comes to foreign affairs. I am no genius but I know that in war those from the other side you keep until the war is over. We call them prisoners of war. I think the Obama administration is forgetting one important thing here. These are not soldiers of war, they are terrorists and their war will never be over so that means they should never be released. They should not be given anything more than what you would someone who committed treason  in a time of war. Do not our soldiers and countrymen  deserve more?

The Pentagon identified the three now former prisoners resettled in Georgia as Abdel Ghaib Ahmad Hakim, Salah Mohammed Salih Al-Dhabi and Abdul Khaled Al-Baydani. The two sent to Slovakia were Hashim Bin Ali Bin Amor Sliti and Husayn Salim Muhammad Al-Mutari Yafai.

Speaking about transparency, what about Bergdahl? How about president Obama stating, "Starting today this administration stands on the side of not those that wish to hold information, but those that seek to make it known." Does not this fall into this category, I am an American I want to know, I served my country I feel I am entitled? Is this guy guilty or innocent? Why hide behind the shadows of manipulation and deception. The president clearly is living in some other world when he stated "The shadow of crisis has past." I guess if you spread peanut butter on burnt toast it won't look like burnt toast anymore.

He stated in the State of the Union, "Will we lead our country wisely using all elements of our power to defeat them and protect us from the next threat?" The next threat is here we are calling it radical Islamism. When he is able to speak these words then maybe we will start to defend our country and then I feel sorry for those who oppose us. He stated also, "Will we allow ourselves to be sorted by fashions and turn against one another?" Well he is the one that spoke about being black and sympathizing with those who protested in rage demolishing the town of Ferguson both physically and emotionally. President Obama has done nothing but confirm what a true politician is.

They say it is not the uniform but the man in the uniform that makes the man. I couldn't agree with this more. Anyone can wear a suit but you can't wear character, it wears you.

# **Wal-Mart splurges**

I love shopping at Wal-Mart, I guess I am that, git er done type guy. I seen on the news tonight that Wal-Mart is going to cash tax refund checks if you do them in their stores. I know it is all a strategy to get people to come into their stores and spend their hard earned money. I understand opportunity, but is it really opportunity or is it slightly taking advantage of peoples spontaneous urges?

Would we call this ethical behavior that we Americans should be proud of? Well after you have been warned, it is then in your hands. You know going in to a store like Wal-Mart there is always one thing you will see you want.

**What if** Wal-Mart made you wait  twenty four hours before you can spend the money.

**What if** Wal-Mart gave you fifty percent off anything you buy in the store up to the amount of your refund? Why does any of this even matter? I guess to me it is about people being taken advantage of.
 If you are going to do it at least make it where everyone wins. Maybe we could call it Obama Shares. What if we deleted words like credit cards, debt, and spend and replaced them with words like budget, save and economize.
I know this is America, so let me get back to shopping and you get back to reading my book. I'm not going to tell you how to handle your money and the government shouldn't either.

## <u>State of the Union</u>

President Obama takes time to be interviewed after the State of the Union. One of those Interviewees were with Glozell, who is a comedian. Are you serious Our president is going to take time out of his busy work schedule to be interviewed by none other than a woman bathing in a bathtub full of milk and fruit-loops. I guess this is just another example I had been talking about where he leaves no space for professionalism. I would have rather he skipped the interview and went golfing, he would have at least looked distinguished and consistent.

I bet France is thinking right now I wish we would have thought of the fruit-loops. Maybe president Obama could get with Kellogg's, Post, or General Mills and we could come up with a new cereal with shapes of terrorists and we could bite their heads off while we eat a well balanced meal. I am just being sarcastic, that would be like eating junk food.

I know comedians have done things with the presidents before but timing is everything. If I were from France I would be pissed thinking he had time to talk to a woman eating fruit- loops in a bathtub, but he didn't have time to stand and support our allies who had been victimized by radical Islamic terrorism. In the State of the Union he hardly mentioned it.

**What if** we make him address it? Does he not still answer to us?

On the other hand if you think about president Obama spending time with Miss Fruit-Loops I think it just shows how he doesn't really take his job that serious. I guess we just wait for the next election when we have an opportunity to upgrade.

## Hillary Clinton's opinion

Hillary Rodham Clinton, has so far avoided taking a position on the Keystone XL pipeline issue. Hillary Clinton is the leading Democratic contender to succeed Obama if she decides to run for president, which many believe she will do. She is the former U.S. Secretary of State.

To date, Hillary Clinton has stayed neutral on whether the U.S. should allow construction of the TransCanada Corp. pipeline, which would carry more than eight hundred thousand barrels of crude oil a day from Alberta and the U.S.

The House has already approved it and the Senate is now considering it. President Obama has vowed to veto the bill as long as the State Department is still conducting a formal review of the project. Clinton has said previously that it would be inappropriate for her to comment on whether the pipeline project should move ahead, given her past role as Obama's top diplomat and the State Department's ongoing assessment. During one interview Hillary spoke on the subject as she clearly avoided taking sides as she seemed to try to speak for both sides, being careful she didn't lose any future votes that she will need later on.

I understand that is politics, but when will we get someone in Washington that's not afraid to not only voice their true opinion but follow through with it.

**What if** we could fire any of these people on their falsifying future expectations?

**What if** America said enough is enough. I understand they would just find another way to pass the blame while making themselves look honorable. The battle comes down to saving our environment, or taking control of the oil prices. I agree both sides do have concerns but **what if** we made them both work together?

## Tennessee standards

A Tennessee school district is looking at lowering the standards on grades so those that might and will fail, could and should pass. They make the argument that if the students do not pass they will drop out of the schools anyway. They will then become welfare recipients and future residents of the correctional institute of society, or at least this increases their odds.

On the other hand we can argue that they have no faith in their own Tennesseans. Are we not shortening the finish line before it has even begun?

If you lower the standards, you encourage lower expectations.

If you encourage lower expectations, you will have to justify ignorance later on, along with accountability that too will be shifted from them back to those who enabled them.

This teaches them that they need just the bare minimum, along with expecting second chances that shouldn't just be given without extenuating circumstances.

While it is commendable, creative and noble, it's just not justifiable, realistic, or honest.

**What if** we let them graduate with less than honorable grades and some of them want to become teachers? How could you tell them they can't when you passed them, encouraging them to go for their dreams. If you then pass them they will then become our future teachers who are less than qualified which will once again lower our standards even more. I am fifty two years old I am still learning. I have yet to see the finish line. I think we should unite to help those who are struggling, rather than enable them by taking tests with grades already on them.

## Our children will reach only as high as we make them.

# **Offensive names**

We live in a world today, where sometimes it's hard to tell the kids from the adults. I remember growing up listening to kids call me names and I called them names as well. I guess that is just kids being kids. At some point though we all grew up having learned that name calling was hurtful and mean.

I remember my mom saying 'Sticks and stones may break my bones, but names will never hurt me." In reality names do hurt emotionally, but again it is an experience that you use to build your own character. These names may have been used to tease and torment without the child ever realizing the true nature of pain it may have caused.

The names I want to talk about are the ones that don't hurt or offend, well unless you are the few, the ten percent of every situation. We have teams like the Atlanta braves, or the Kansas city Chiefs, whose names have offended those of the Indian heritage. Next we will have the Minnesota Twins whose name will offend twins from around the world and the Saint Lewis Cardinals, I'm sure will offend the Pope. We have KFC that was once known as Kentucky Fried Chicken. Now this name changed not because it offended anyone, but because it was a business issue. It was about money — money that Kentucky Fried Chicken would have had to pay to continue using their original name.

In 1990, the Commonwealth of Kentucky, mired in debt, took the unusual step to trademark their name. preventing, anyone using the word "Kentucky" for business reasons, inside or outside of the state they would have to obtain permission and pay licensing fees to the Commonwealth of Kentucky. It was to lessen government debt, but it was also one that isolated one of the most famous companies Kentucky Fried Chicken.

## To tackle or not to tackle

Clarence Daniels sixty two years old was tackled going into the Wal-Mart store in Florida by a person who observed Clarence Daniels with a gun under his jacket. The person who tackled him believed he was there to cause harm. If he would have been there to do harm then everyone would be looking at Michael Foster who was forty three years old as a hero, but instead he tackled someone who was legally carrying in a State that is known for stand your own ground.

**What if** Clarence Daniels would have felt threatened and then shot Michael Foster?

I think this was an interesting case because, what did we learn?

**What if** Michael Foster would have been a bad guy? By exposing your gun in the open carry you allow the bad guys to make the first move and not just the first move but towards you.

I think the whole thing was handled correctly and I think Michael Foster was meaning to do good. Hopefully he will learn from it as well and he will not get any tough fine out of it. It is a little surprising that in a State that is so well known for its stand your own ground, it didn't cross his mind that the guy was carrying legally.

**To be aware of your surroundings is the first step to survival.**

## Jury selection

Picking a jury is never easy no matter what the case is about. For the trial of Dzhokhar Tsarnaev. Who is in court over the Boston marathon bombing, there has been some jurors that are on opposite sides of the death penalty. One in particular doesn't think there is any evidence that would prove the suspected bomber is or could be innocent, while another can't imagine convicting someone to death, just on their own beliefs.

Jury selection is done using lawyers from both sides to ask the hard questions and challenge those that may have alternative motives or extreme opinions. A 1985 ruling from the U.S. Supreme Court said a juror can lawfully be excused if his views on the death penalty are so strong that they would prevent or substantially impair his ability to follow the law. On the other side, they argue that death-qualified juries do not represent a true cross-section of the community and are less likely to be understanding, or concerned to the defenses side.

Trial cases are about one thing as far as the lawyers are concerned which is winning. The courts are there to seek justice pushing a fare and impartial trial that everyone will walk away satisfied. Very few cases, do both sides truly feel satisfied.

**What if** you let half the jurors be for and the other half against and then you only have to sway one for or against.

**What if** we trust our lawyers to put the best people on the panel and accept their choices?

## Justice is for all, rich, poor, famous and not so famous.

## Befriending a foreigner

A former Navy seal Marcus Lutrell who was fighting in Afghanistan, had come under fire losing everyone in his unit. He was the last and he was wounded and alone or so he thought he was. As the terrorists were closing in so was another Afghanistan resident called Mohammed Gulab he was a goat herder who was trying to warn Lutrell but they did not understand him.

He came to Lutrell's rescue saving one of our own. Mohammed Gulab has since come and visited a few times with Marcus Lutrell and is seeking asylum here in the USA. The Department of Homeland Security will ultimately make the decision as to whether or not to grant Gulab asylum, but at this time, the agency has not yet made a comment one way or the other.

Why have they not yet made a decision? Marcus Lutrell is a former navy seal who has a purple heart and Navy cross for his actions. His actions along with Mohamed Gulab were quick and decisive saving our American soldier's life and preventing him from being captured and tortured.

**What if** Mohammed Gulab is turned away with no where safe to live?

**What if** we get in another battle but this time the goat herder knows he will not be given safe haven here. Do you think he is going to risk his own life?

**What if** we treat Mohammed Gulab better than we treat our illegal aliens, and that's pretty good. They are here sleeping in our country right now, and they did it illegally. Not like Mohammed Gulab who wants to do things the right way.

**What if** we look at this as a way to bring two nations together one person at a time.

## Judge veto's babies name

A Judge ruled against naming a baby Nutella, which we all know as the chocolate hazelnut spread. Nutella is delicious to some, but would you name your child after it? A baby in the French city of Valenciennes was recently named for the chocolate-hazelnut spread, but a local judge renamed her Ella after ruling that the moniker Nutella wasn't in the child's best interest.

A number of countries have long had laws protecting kids against seemingly odd names. "In France, Napoleon outlawed names that might subject a child to ridicule." New Zealand has pretty strict naming laws, you can't use names that are generally titles or honorifics, like Prince, King, or Princess, which are becoming more popular in the U.S."

I guess here in the United states we are safe, unless we start talking about names of sports teams, or businesses that want others to change their names for various reasons. They talk about names that may harm a child or make fun of them.

Let us look at some names from the past and see if we might not think those names were just as weird.

Viviette, Anthea, Doretta, Bernadine, Hecuba, Arthurette. Are you going to tell me none of these names seem, weird? So if we see them as weird, why are we the ones that get punished?

**What if** we were told what name to name our children? I guess that is why we live here, in the USA land of the free.

## To thank America is to respect America

# CHAPTER SIX

## <u>Fighters</u>

Americans, we are fighters, We are not afraid to take a stand. We have been doing it since before we came to this country. We told the world we are Americans and we were moving to our own country. We fight for equal rights and against slavery, sexual discrimination is not wanted here. We have those that want to strip us of our right to bear arms. There are some fighting for legalizing  abortion and others for banning illegal citizens.

Proud Americans fight for what they believe in, whether it is just a few fighting for what they feel is important, or the many who wish to keep our country in check. I hope you have liked some of the topics we have covered here so far.

# "What if"

## Uncle Sam wants you

**To stand up and fight for freedom and democracy
Let your voice be heard.**

## <u>ICE is melting</u>

ICE was created in 2003 through a merger of the investigative and interior enforcement elements of the former U.S. Customs Service and the Immigration and Naturalization Service. ICE now has more than 20,000 employees in more than 400 offices in the United States and 48 foreign countries.
They have a budget near 6 million dollars annually used for Homeland Security Investigations and Enforcement and Removal Operations.

What is Enforcement and Removal Operations (ERO) mission? It is to identify, arrest, and remove aliens who present a danger to national security or are a risk to public safety, as well as those who enter the United States illegally or otherwise undermine the integrity of our immigration laws and our border control efforts. Enforcement and Removal Operations (ERO) upholds America's immigration laws at, within and beyond our borders through efficient enforcement and removal operations. This information came from the U.S. Immigration and Customs Enforcement web page.

**What if** we ask some questions now?
How many illegal Immigrants are shipped out of this country annually?
How many are released back in our communities after they have been identified?

**What if** we look at the procedure for removing them from our country?

Where does that 6 million dollars get distributed to in detail? To which offices and their locations. Is this not one of the agencies under President Obama who he had mentioned earlier on transparency?

I think he said the following
"I am giving my administration on, how to interpret the Freedom of Information Act. For a long time there has been too much secrecy in this city.

Starting today every agency and department should know that this administration  stands on the side of not those that seek to hold information, but those that seek to make it known."

It's time to hold these agencies accountable. Let them show us what they have accomplished.

**What if** these agencies create so many departments within their agencies it is easier to push the blame around from one department to another when their department comes under fire?

In defense of the ICE agency I will say Ronald Belciano a drug trafficker  received more than 5 years in federal prison for money laundering and drug trafficking. Over 3 million dollars was seized.

In 2014 alone, ICE's Homeland Security Investigations (HSI) initiated 987 human trafficking investigations and recorded 1,770 arrests, 1,028 indictments, 828 convictions associated to human trafficking and identified 440 victims.
I praise the agency on this.

I know they do not answer to me, so my praise may mean very little, but I am still an American one of many and they do answer to all of us.

Accountability should be expected as part of the check and balance system to all agencies, it's nothing personal it's just a safety precaution to see everyone is working together

**What if** we put Immigration on ice?

## <u>Defining Terrorists</u>

Finally we are getting somewhere with the White House. It seemed like there was a breakdown in communications, when it came to talking about terrorists and radical Islamists. I never knew there was a difference between Terrorists and armed insurgencies, but according to the White House Spokesman Eric Schultz there is a difference.

When Eric Schultz was asked why the United States opposes Jordan's decision to seek a prisoner swap, he explained that Isis were terrorist and we do not negotiate with them. The Taliban on the other hand is not a terrorist organization. They are armed insurgents And stated we are trying to bring an end to the war implying by releasing them all will be ended.

**Insurgent** is a person who fights against an established government, or authority.

**Insurgency** a usual violent attempt to take control of the government.

**Terrorist** is a person who uses terrorism in the pursuit of political aim. Now that we have these translations let us look at Isis and the Taliban to understand them better.

**Taliban** A suicide bomber struck a funeral in Afghanistan for the victims of an earlier Taliban attack, killing 16 people and wounding 39, an Afghan official reported. The attack took place in eastern Laghman province, according to the local governor's spokesman, Sarhadi Zwak. No one immediately claimed responsibility for the bombing but the blame is likely to fall on the Taliban who have staged similar attacks in the past.

The district of Sayed Abad in Wardak province east of the capital, Kabul, Taliban fighters dragged two villagers from their home and killed them, according to spokesman Attaullha Khugyani.

The Pentagon has released five Yemeni detainees from a high-security prison in Guantanamo Bay, Cuba, and sent them to Oman and Estonia. They are terrorists and they are Taliban.

## Can you tell who is Taliban and who is Isis?

**Isis** has been involved in countless attacks, beheading many civilians and children, along with Christian persecution with no regard for age or gender. We need to stop playing games. We are Americans and we are fed up with your branding the average American as naïve.

The White house is testing our ability to compare paper towels to napkins, or Kleenex to tissue, a vehicle to an automobile. How about a politician to a liar? A terrorist is a terrorist so call it anything you like but understand, for us to listen to you is for us to believe in you, so tell the truth. Isis and the Taliban have and are waging war on America and her allies using terrorist style assaults.

One of the five Taliban released has already been said to have returned to the battlefield. Rear Admiral John Kirby stated that the Defense Department is comfortable with monitoring these individuals and any terrorist activities?

Why would they need to monitor them for terrorist activities when they stated earlier they are not terrorists, they are armed insurgents? Remember what I said earlier once you tell one lie then you have to tell another one. Maybe the press secretary should swear on a bible before he speaks publicly, along with any of the other White House staff.

# S.O.S./ 911

First Lieutenant Clint Lorance was found guilty of two
counts of murder in the 2012 killing of two suspected
Taliban fighters. In a remote sector of Kandahar
Province Afghanistan. Lieutenant Clint Lorance was
sentenced to twenty years in Leavenworth. The
prosecution stated that the Lieutenant ordered his men
to open fire on unarmed civilians, using his rank and
position to intimidate and harass. The prosecuting
attorney was Captain William Miller. The defense
stated that they were in a hostile environment and that
all the known civilians had left due to the volatile
danger that illuminated the area. First Lieutenant Clint
Lorance had just taken over command as the platoon
had suffered several losses including the commander.

On July 2nd 2012 headed to a remote village within the
Kandahar sector of Afghanistan for a combat patrol on
foot. His patrol which consisted of sixteen U.S. Soldiers
and five Afghan National Army Soldiers. He was being
fed information from above by U.S. helicopter pilots
informing him of the enemy on the North, East and
West sides of their platoon. Who would charge one of
our own Soldiers as a murderer while they fought for
our country in a combat zone?

**What if** we investigate this closer? Were the civilians shot actually proven to be civilians? Was Lieutenant Clint Lorance where he was supposed to be?

**What if** you were in the same situation would you had done the same thing? Do you think if you were in another country  where it was hard to tell who was friendly and who was not, you wouldn't be nervous, especially after you had just lost soldiers days before?

Why is president Obama not looking at helping out this soldier who was willing to go fight for his country.

**What if** we are trying to tell our soldiers that you will do time if you mess up?

**What if** president Obama is using this as a deterrent to scare away our future soldiers with threats of lifelong consequences, so as to acquire political gains while reducing our military support?

Save our soldiers from political fire, they along with their families have sacrificed enough already.

**What if** we stop talking about transparency and become transparent?

## First Lieutenant Clint Lorance, may the truth set you free.

## <u>Excluded for enabling</u>

In Hartford Connecticut  The gunman, Adam Lanza, began his rampage on Dec. 14, 2012, by killing Nancy Lanza inside their Newtown home before gunning down 26 people at Sandy Hook Elementary School and then killing himself.  The Newtown massacre debate on whether the victims counted in the dedication should include the shooter's mother, a woman who has been faulted for contributing to the tragedy by fostering her son's fascination with guns.

The commissioner Harold Schwartz asked at a hearing on  why Nancy Lanza should not also be considered a victim, she was the mother of said shooter.

I understand where this issue becomes controversial, It is putting the name of the killers mother on anything with the victims. To them they want to hand out their own form of punishment by excluding her from the dedication. Having listened to their side you now also have to listen to her side the mother Nancy Lanza who at this moment can't speak to the victims, well actually she can speak to those that are with her in heaven, but for all the surviving victims I'm sure she would say she was sorry.

**What if** we ask a few questions? Before excluding her. Did she not too become a victim by her own son? Was her death any less tragic? Did she train her son knowingly and willingly to go kill all these victims?

I understand if a robber gets shot while committing a crime or evading the police with a gun in their hand that this becomes a natural consequence when they get shot and possibly killed, but what crime did she commit?

Is it that she let her son go shooting at a target range, which is perfectly legal? Were there issues of her isolating her son from the rest of the world? Was she too then not isolated from the world herself making her a victim also? What constitutes a victim? The definition according to the dictionary, it is a person harmed, injured, or killed as a result of a crime accident, or other event or action. Just under the definition itself she was all that.

Did she enable her son through neglect, or was she giving her son all the mothering skills she had available? Do you think God will punish her for what her son did? If God will forgive her shouldn't we? Are any of us higher than He himself who makes all the true and final decisions?

In regards to all the victims I am sorry for your losses and can never truly understand your personal feelings on each of your losses, but I do understand losing someone close by murder. There is a grieving time we must all have to go through and each one of us will process differently taking more or less time as needed. Some will cry where others will hold their tears inside never sharing. I only ask that whatever decision you make you at least look at the mother and ask was she not a victim too, did she not suffer the loss of her son, her life and most of all the lives of many innocent and helpless people that I'm sure she too loved?

## **Deflate Gate**

Today is the Sunday of all Sundays, for this year. It is Super Bowl Forty Nine and two teams The New England Patriots and Seattle Seahawks are ready to battle it out on the field, goal post to goal post to see who will reign as champion.

 While they battle on the field of green and white, others will be battling behind the scenes, to keep things right The debate on deflate remains a worthwhile controversy on both sides. Let us look at the arguments to see if we can deflate any discrepancies in their arguments.

On the one side you have to ask, does it really matter? Apparently it must have some sequential importance, as all the balls were tested and all the balls came into below regulation standards. If it didn't matter it would not have even been brought up as a concern.

On the other side of the ball, they think it is of minimal value. To them it just comes down to the better team and better plays.

**What if** we look at the kicker. Does he not have certain people that hold the ball for him? Does he want the ball angled a certain way? Does the wind influence him on the way he kicks the ball? So why could it not be possible for a quarterback to be able to throw and grip the ball that has less air in it better? To you and me it may not make a difference but to a seasoned professional, who has thrown thousands of balls it could make all the difference in the world. If it's cold outside would a soft ball maybe sting less?

**What if** we change the rules where the only balls used are the ones the NFL issue and not the teams themselves. No team will have an advantage this way.

**What if** we use one ball a designated amount of time no matter whether you are on offense or defense, when the time is up you change balls. This would keep everything fare as both quarterbacks would be using the same ball.

Well Super Bowl forty Nine is over and the Patriots beat Seattle. It came down to judgment and opportunity, along with perseverance. What will be the next excuse to challenge the NFL? Both teams played hard, but interceptions and turnovers were present during the game.

Were they due to deflated balls this time? I think not. It came down to decision making, ball control and time management, along with perseverance. Yes opportunity was there and some players took advantage of that. With the exception of the second to last play that turned into a Pro Wrestling match

I think the game was great. Though we may now have our next controversy sportsman like conduct. Let's see if they just ignore the skirmish and blow it off as everyone was all pumped up. Here we go from deflated to all pumped up.

## **Selfies Banned**

I guess it is true taking a picture can cause serious bodily injury. A polish woman on vacation Teetering on the ledge of the Puente de Triana bridge in the city of Seville. Sylwia Rajchel was a medical student she was 23 years old, as she tried to take a photo of herself, she slipped and fell 15 feet onto the concrete footings of the structure.

This was not the only case in August, a couple fell from the rocky edge of a cliff in Cabo da Raca, Portugal while trying to take a photo of themselves on the edge. Why am I bringing this up now since this is not in the United States?

Because the way our country is headed I might as well address this before it gets here. I know there are many cities overseas banning selfies.

**What if** we think about this?

**What if** we again hold each person accountable for their own actions, instead of punishing everyone for the spontaneous few? Maybe we could teach classes on the proper way to take selfies so no one gets injured.

**What if** we focus on educating rather than banning?

Just remember I told you so. We already got laws against texting and driving. I do agree with that law by the way. It won't be long and someone will bring this to America, so let us just be ready.

Until then, look around your environment before you take any selfies. I highly encourage you to buddy up with someone just for some extra reinsurance. Don't zoom to doom, play it safe, but again it is your call.

## <u>Conspiracy S.B. 49</u>

I guess there is another excuse to challenge the NFL, but what and why? Everyone has an opinion on the game whether or not there were mistakes made on accident, or whether there was a conspiracy on who to give the ball to. Should the star of the game be the quarter back, or the running back? Some mentioned that they did not give the ball to Marshawn Lynch due to trying to keep his contract down lower. Some say that they gave it to the quarterback to make him the MVP of the game.

**What if** it was a conspiracy where someone made a bet throwing the game on purpose for more money from some side bet? Who could control the game? The quarterback could have thrown the ball instead of running it.

The coach could have called the play, the owner could have told the coach what to do, so there are a few scenarios just on that area. We could go back to it being the most important game of the year and in one quick flash the wrong decision was made that others sitting on their couches would have called differently, including me. I do though accept I am only a spectator and I leave the ball handling to the coaches and players. I will remember the game as a close one and one with a few exciting plays. I will also remember the un-sportsman like conduct understanding however that though they were justified with emotions, they were not justified with actions.

**What if** we just hold out our hands and congratulate the winners making us all then winners.

**What "If's",** these are just some of the What "If's" as long as you are looking at everything then you are at least looking open mindedly. That is all this book is about looking at things fairly not making any decision until you have looked at everything.

## Let us get ready for Super Bowl Fifty.

## <u>The Vaccine debate</u>

There is a measles outbreak going on right now and with that, comes the debate on whether or not everyone should be forced to get the virus shot.
Some argue that it causes autism. Not sure where they get their information from, but that is why a few refuse the shot. Others think that if the kids do not get the shots they should not be allowed to go to the schools where they could spread the virus.

**What if** we ask, what is the shot suppose to do here? Because if it doesn't work unless one hundred percent of the population takes the shot than it is not worth taking is it? Is not the person who gets the shot going to be less likely to get the measles and for those that do get the measles won't it be a more mild outbreak?

**What if** each person talks with their own physician and leaves the medical decisions to them. I think anytime the President tries to sale something he looks like a car salesman running a scam. I only say that because he seems to only do everything we don't want.

**What if** this is a conspiracy and there is more to that shot than meets the eye? I understand that when you throw the word conspiracy out there you get people saying not again, but who invented the word conspiracy and why was it invented? When they use the word force on everyone it does make you think someone is desperate, let's just hope it's all for the right reason.

I will most likely take my kids to get the shot, but I do think how things are presented through the media and by whom can help or hurt a cause. Now it's your shot, it's all up to you.

## CHAPTER SEVEN
## In the schools

A nine year old boy bragged to another classmate that he could make him vanish. Aiden Steward was suspended from his elementary school in Kermit, Texas after making the alleged terroristic threat. promising another child he'd render him invisible with his fictional "one ring" from the J.R.R. Tolkien's fantasy series The Lord of the Rings.

His parents stated he was just acting out characters of the different movies The principal Roxanne Greer didn't see it the same way. She issued disciplinary action and told the father threats to another child would not be tolerated. The child has been suspended twice before, once for referring to another student as black, reported by the New York Daily News and once bringing the Big Book of Knowledge" to school, which his teacher reportedly had an issue with because of its illustrations of a pregnant woman.

The Texas Education Code's student code includes suspension as a means of "preventing and intervening in student discipline problems, including bullying, harassment, and making hit lists.

The Big Book of Knowledge has tons of fascinating facts about people, animals, plants, and more! This unique reference offers full-color illustrations, helpful diagrams, fact panels, quizzes, and more, all designed to exercise your mind. Countless topics are featured, including, weather, space travel, sound, trees and plants, along with mammals, reptiles and amphibians.

Here we have one child being punished for wanting to learn? The Big Book of Knowledge is designed for students. I do not understand the thinking. The teacher stated the books showed pictures of a pregnant woman. Are these books inappropriate for these students?

The boy was suspended for referring to another student as black, was he lying?

**What if** at nine years old the boy had an over active imagination?

**What if** we ask was this boy being disruptive or was he just being a normal nine year old boy? I'm not sure that the teacher can even use the word terroristic threat, since our President has yet to identify its true origin. How serious was the boy when he talked of making one vanish?

**What if** we look at whether it is the student, or the administration that may need some adjusting. I cannot say one way or the other but these topics seem bazaar to extreme, as though they are missing common sense.

**Let us not sensor any one from knowledge, but encourage a creative mind.**

## Vacation stay or go

There appears to be a debate on whether children should travel with their parents overseas on vacation.

Some think that the children are too young to experience and appreciate a vacation from a far. There are others that think you should spend your vacation at home spending quality time with your family, while others add the grandparents, relatives and friends into the mix as well.

Some fear going on vacation puts your children and others at risk from diseases upon returning from other countries due to lower standards on vaccines and other elements that factor in.

On the other side there are those that argue stating that exposing children to other cultures, seeing the world, and meeting people in other places makes you a more well-rounded, open-minded, and accepting person. They talked about money being a concern, that some spend money not thinking about saving it for later, such as retirement, or college for the young ones.

**What if** we accept the fact that not everyone sees life the same way, that's why we live in America.

**What if** when those that argue a child is too young to appreciate a vacation, we stop and think.

**What if** it is the parents that want to remember the vacation with their children at a certain young age?

**What if** those that think vacation should be at home with family members playing games and telling stories? We look at what games and what stories? Are they wanting stories about things that only happen in their communities? If they tell stories about people, or adventures from outside their residential area, then why read it when you can live it? Those that are worried about viruses and epidemics being brought back may have some legitimate concerns.

But **what if** those that travel abroad  do enough studying and researching to know what dangers and issues of importance are out there. Some may think they want to travel now and later will lose interest.

**What if** you decide to wait till later  and you get to sick , or too old to go on your life hood dream?

**What if** those that don't think traveling abroad is a good thing? You could travel around our magnificent country. If you like beaches there are the coast line states. If you like the mountains we have areas that are filled with splendor and awe.

There is the Yellow Stone National Park, Grand Canyon, Las Vegas, Disneyland, Disney World, There is Texas and the Alamo

These places have fun and history included in them.

**What if** we just leave the final decision to those that have worked to earn a vacation and worked to raise their own families. I do think that all those issues are legitimate.

**What if** we take other relatives along on vacation? There are lots of different options sometimes getting away from family is a vacation as well.

Whatever you decide I am sure you will make the best decision for you and your family, I hope you enjoy your next vacation and don't forget to take lots of pictures.

To say you were there, is better than saying you have never been.

To wonder upon a dream, when you could have fulfilled it.

## All choices point back to you.

## **Jordan Retaliates**

Jordan hanged two Iraqi jihadists, one a woman, on Wednesday in response to an Islamic State video showing a captured Jordanian pilot being burnt alive by the group Isis. The woman, Sajida al-Rishawi, was one that Isis was wanting to barter for in exchange for a Japanese hostage whom they later beheaded. Sentenced to death for her role in a 2005 suicide bomb attack in Amman, Rishawi was executed at dawn, a security source and state television said.

Jordan, which is part of the U.S.-led alliance against Islamic State, has promised an "earth-shaking response" to the killing of its pilot, Mouath al-Kasaesbeh, who was captured in December when his F-16 warplane crashed over northeastern Syria.

I hope President Obama is watching this with his eyes wide open, in fact I hope America is watching this with their eyes wide open. We know that the President always seems to blink or look away in times of turmoil.

Let us watch this closely to see how Isis will respond. I like the you kill one of ours, we kill ten of yours. Two was a good start though. We need to get a grip on this. If President Obama thinks he can't follow through, there is no shame in relinquishing his power and authority to the betterment of our country.

I am glad finally someone took a stand, enough is enough I only hope we can follow our allies who seem to be the ones leading us. The question is will we be there for them when they need us, or will we turn tail and run? Actions speak louder than words. No matter how you wish to spin this you still have to answer to the question, where were we when we were needed most?

## **Smoking Confessions**

Wow, Senator Cruz and Jeb Bush both admitted to smoking pot when they were younger. Is this good to know? Should we be mad at them for waiting so long to tell us? I think it is great they admitted to doing something wrong and have since learned from it. I think that is a good trait to have when you can admit your own mistakes. When you lie and deceive to present yourself as anything other than what you are, that is where your true character comes out and tells the American people you can or cannot be trusted.

I have never smoked pot and not sure how many others are out there with me, but I know more people that have, than have not, or at least so they have said. Even Bill Clinton was said to have smoked just not inhaled. So was Hillary with him, because if she were and he didn't inhale it had to go somewhere, makes you think twice after that statement.

If we are legalizing pot in Colorado which is one of our States. For those residence who smoke it currently, then I think we should allow those that did it in the past that are no longer doing it to run for offices.

I have no problem with those who smoked it in the past most of us were teenagers at one time or another. I tried regular cigarettes but never liked them thank God I never got hooked.

It all comes down not so much as someone's past, as it does to someone's intensions for the future. If nothing else this is a topic that needs to be aired out in more ways than one.

## <u>Second chance gun</u>

This week, five instructors for the Missouri city's police department are training to use a "less lethal" device, called the Alternative, this gun has enough force to knock a suspect to the ground without killing them.

The Alternative is a small orange device that attaches to the top of a normal handgun and extends a Ping-Pong-ball-sized projectile in front of the muzzle. The Missouri police are looking for less lethal devices, question is will this cause more confusion and controversies?

**What if** they add this new weapon to their arsenal and get in a conflict Now they have their gun, this new device, their Taser and more choices which may also make them slower to react because now they have to decide which one to use.

**What if** the seamlessly routine stop, escalates quickly and you grab the wrong weapon?

**What if** you shoot someone never having pulled the other device, will that not add tension making those who oppose the law already try to manipulate the courts.

**What if** this device was available during the Michael Brown shooting do you think he would still have gotten shot?

I understand and applaud there trying to create alternative ways as long as they don't take away the edge that the officer will need to arrest and apprehend.

## Respect the badge but fear the gun

## <u>Deceit in the News</u>

Brian Williams one of the most watched News Anchormen in America. He recently confessed he had lied. He stated that he was shot down by enemy fire in Iraq, only to later come back and recant his statement. He then stated he was in the helicopter following one that had been shot down stating he spent two harrowing nights in a sand storm in Iraq. There was a pilot who stated Brian Williams asked him what happened, referring that maybe he was not even there. Others had stated as soon as their helicopter landed they left the area to a safer destination.

I do not think his apology was sincere. It appeared as though even through trying to correct his statement he was minimizing, while trying to still look heroic. To me there is nothing heroic about a liar.

It takes a lifetime to build a reputation but only a minute on national TV to ruin one.

**What if** he would just have come out and said sorry. I lied about being shot down on a helicopter, it never really happened.

**What if** no one truly believes anything he reports anymore?

**What if** these are the reasons that the media sometimes comes under attack for false reporting?

**What if** we repeat what the news reports and we find out later they were wrong, who's liable?

There is talk whether he will keep his job or will be fired, laid off, or quietly moved to another position. I can only speak for myself, if I were to watch him on the news I would change the channel for one reason, I want the news that I can rely on, I want the truth. If the news is reported by anyone other than an honest person it becomes tainted and fictitious. It is then no longer news it is just a story. I have no problem with stories, but that is not the purpose America watches the news.

If he were reporting in Ferguson, Mo what would you believe after knowing this about him? What would we think about anything he reported? Brian Williams most watched News Anchorman is now the news, hope the one reporting on him is honest. I do not hate the guy and yes he made a mistake, but he is just doing patch work till all is forgotten.

## **Declaring War**

I was watching Fox News today, actually I watch it every day. They were talking about what it takes to declare war. They stated four ways that we could declare war. Let us look at these four ways.

<u>Number one</u>, if a country or entity attacks the United States in any one of our fifty States

<u>Number two,</u> if a country or entity is about to attack the United States in any of our fifty States

<u>Number three,</u> if an enemy of a friendly country is attacked without provocation, they may ask us to assist them with military aid, which could be money, support troops, weapons and supplies. It could be reconnaissance or intelligence.

<u>Number four,</u> If the United States is in a treaty that obligates us to declare war according to the terms set in place.

The President does however have other means. He has a slush fund account with the pentagon and it is all legal. They mentioned that if we are attacked overseas we do not have the right to declare war. Does this then mean our soldiers who are and have fought for us have no true protection? Our bases overseas that are faithfully guarded by our American soldiers, do they not represent America?

### **Fighting there so we don't have to here.**

# **Bar Shots**

After a mother's son has come up missing leaving a bar. Law makers are wanting to make it mandatory that cameras be posted outside all bars. In the bill, the bars would have to pay half of the cost and the city would pick up the other half.

A debate is already starting on both sides. Those that are opposed to it, state it violates the fourth amendment, the right to privacy. They mentioned questions like who owns the tapes? At what point can the tapes be accessed and would a court order be needed? Discrimination then becomes an issue as well, for why should bars have to pay for the cameras when there are businesses all around them that wouldn't have to? Should it not be as much the responsibilities of these other businesses as well?

**What if** it just came down to privacy, how could you plead the fifth if they have you on camera?

**What if** it was just about who had to pay for it. You could have the city pay for it up front and then collect not from the bars but from the person who committed the crime. They argue that they are, referring to the bars are responsible for their patrons. If this is true then who is responsible when we enter restaurants, Movie theaters, churches, schools, or the malls? Who watches over us at night when we are in our own homes asleep?

Instead of setting up surveillance, because that is really what the purpose of the cameras are intended for, we patrol more in those areas where crime may occur in peak hours. The cameras may deter someone from committing a crime or it may just postpone them from committing a crime in that area due to the current scenario.

If they make it law that they have to use cameras, is the camera going to be ordered to stay on twenty four seven, or just during the hours of businesses? Is the camera going to be ordered to be continually focused? Who determines where the camera gets placed and who does maintenance on it when it breaks down? Who pays for the tapes and store them? Does the city hold on to the tapes they pay for or does the owner of the bar?

**What if** we use law enforcement, detectives, witnesses, and forensics?

## Obama Preaches

On Thursday, President Barack Obama seized the opportunity of the National Prayer Breakfast to speak frankly, criticizing the "terrible deeds" ...committed "in the name of Christ."

"Humanity has been grappling with these questions throughout human history," Obama stated. "And lest we get on our high horse and think this is unique to some other place, remember that during the Crusades and the Inquisition, people committed terrible deeds in the name of Christ.

**What if** President Obama explained about the terrible acts that Isis is committing currently instead of reversing the focus on the terrible acts that were committed from a long time ago? No act of violence should be excused, but on that note it should never be one sided either. He is quick to yell Christianity while he whispers Radical Extremist in an area no one hears or sees his lips move, Hmm, why is that?

**What if** Obama just wants to go through the motions while never stopping to deal with any issue in true form?

**What if** President Obama told us what he learned when he went to Reverend Wright's ministry since he wishes to bring up Christianity?

## <u>Cover Story</u>

The First Lady has been chosen to pose for the cover of Cooking Light magazine. In its near thirty years they have never had a person grace the cover of their magazine. Her let's move program has been going on for close to five years. Has it been successful? I don't know, but she has stayed firm on her stance to fight for healthier foods and exercise.

They showed pictures of her with others gardening. My question is how much is real and how much is fake? You see the picture of her in the black and white outfit looks too nice to want to work in unless just for a photo shoot.

If she is real on this and this is not just another Obama prop, then I think it is great. America should want its citizens to live healthier.

**What if** the First Lady addressed food stamps?

**What if** other programs were monitored so as to see where best to place the funds?

**What if** the First Lady explained her daily exercises so we would have some sort of knowledge on her let's move program?

The lets move program consisted of five steps let's look at them.

**#1**, Move a minimum of sixty minutes a day. I could do this from the couch so is this really even worthy of being considered an exercise program? Kids have tons of energy but if you set low expectations you achieve low results.

**#2** Try a new fruit, or vegetable they say there are thousands of fruits that many have never tried. Do they mean thousands in our local area, or are they referring to around the world where many fruits and vegetables don't have to meet the same food and safety standards as they would back here? What about how you get some foods from another country here, just the costs could be ridiculously high.

**#3** Drink lots of water and slack off the sodas. I agree with this one, but again how much of this really is the move and how much is really just common sense?

**#4** Do jumping jacks to break up time. So  do these jumping jacks fall in under the sixty minutes or are they under additional time?

**#5** Making dinner is the fifth one, but to me it is only reaffirming the hunger state. After doing all the other things now you are going to hang out in the kitchen, where your mind speaks to your stomach and you may get hungry eat a lot and the cycle continues.

## Fifty shades goes black and white

The National Center on Sexual Exploitation is battling the release of the movie Fifty Shades of Grey, stating it just glamorizes violence against women. So is this group and other groups alike, against all movies that depict violence no matter what, or just women?

**What if** they are violent movies on the mafia, or gangs?

**What if** we look at the monster movies like Friday the thirteenth, exorcist, or westerns?

 Fifty Shades is a movie for entertainment purposes only. Why not look at the audience? Why is it that most the ones that want to see the movie are the ones that they say are victims? Maybe they are all in denial or else they just want to enjoy the sins on the screen.

As a writer I know the whole idea is to captivate your audience, some do it through humor, fear, adrenalin, sex, or intellectual knowledge. When you open a book and sense yourself falling inside the book becoming one of the characters, or being attached to a topic, then the book has served its purpose.

For any group to band together to exterminate a book from existence falls in to violating the first amendment right, freedom of speech. For those that are against the violence do not go see the movie you will be better for not doing so, since your purpose of watching the movie would be full of pain watching women be dominated, while others may watch the movie fantasizing on who they wish they were in the movie.

## Textbook Error

A father in Florida is upset with his child's school. The school is forcing it's students to recite a part of the Quran which is equivalent to the Christian version of the Ten Commandments. This is out of the <u>Florida's Teachers Edition textbook</u>, which is the same book that is missing over a hundred pages that were dedicated to the Christianity and Judaism.

**What if** we look at this closer? Where are these pages at? Why would they spend the money on books that were missing over a hundred pages? Why is it the only pages missing were the other religions?

**What if** we ask the teacher and faculty some questions? Why would you force your students to study Islamic material while denying them the right to study Christian or Judaism. If you state there was a misprint in the text book don't use it? Would you use a math book if it were missing a hundred pages? How could you add and subtract if you are missing key pages in your math book describing the math formulas? Or in science? Would you feel comfortable mixing two chemicals together knowing you are missing the pages in between that tell what the action may be or the amount of a certain chemical? What about history? What if you are missing a hundred pages in history, that can cover a lot of years, that is enough to alter the history of a century?

Doesn't this seem a little suspicious, especially with all the Muslim controversy going on in the world today?

**What if** we get Michele Obama on this, we could fit this in to her (Let's Move program). We start with getting the school to move and round up all those books and mail them back then tell the printing company to move and reprint the books correctly as they were intended to be printed in the first place. This would make for a healthier subject that was complete and well balanced providing all the mental nutrition our children would need to grow and maintain a healthy life style.

If the Muslims can have their book
Why can't the Christians have theirs?

# The forgotten Lie

It would be unjust to forget about Hillary Clinton, after we had put Brian Williams under such scrutiny, not that he didn't deserve it. When Hillary R. Clinton was the First Lady she spoke knowingly lying to all of us about being under sniper fire, while visiting Tuzla, Bosnia, in March 1996. She stated " I remember landing under sniper fire. There was suppose to be some kind of greeting ceremony at the air port, but instead we just ran with our heads down to get to our vehicles to get to our base."

She then could not even admit she lied once she got caught, but instead blamed it on sleep deprivation. I guess she thinks we are all ignorant to her. Are politicians that far out of touch with society that they think we will believe anything they say? A picture is worth a thousand words and there are lots of pictures that disputed not just the events but if you look at Hillary Clinton you will see she at no time looked sleep deprived but rather alert and chipper greeting all eagerly.

**What if** we go ahead and believe her, challenging her ability to run as President of the United States by her own words? If she stated she misspoke under sleep deprivation, then what will she do as President with less sleep and more responsibility?

**What if** we hold all those we trust to lead us to the simple standards of trust, honesty and accountability?

**What if** we start reviewing her past to catch her lies? I am sure anyone that tells such a tall tale of being shot at by snipers has other lies as well.

**What if** we look at the Benghazi story, could there be similar results here when we ask who really knew about this? Let's not forget her words "What difference at this point does it make?" If she wants to be President who will she debate and how will she debate them, she cannot argue who can you trust she would lose. She cannot argue she is more qualified, I guess she could do that but that would only tell me we were in a lot of trouble.

**What if** we just keep it real, let's not waste our time debating with liars. Let us be the first to set the standards high enough we eliminate the liars one by one. We Americans want the truth. If she can't take owner ship for her own words, why do you think we would be comfortable with her speaking for us on our behalf?

I am not going to risk my reputation I have worked so hard maintaining, to let a liar speak for me no thank you. I think I can speak for myself, I guess I am doing that right now writing this book. Let's not even look at the example she set as a mother lying in front of her daughter on TV.

# CHAPTER EIGHT

## The Yoga cover up

A Montana lawmaker says yoga pants should be illegal in public. Republican Senator David Moore is looking to introduce a Bill that would eliminate them being worn in public along with the showing of any nipple including men. Any clothing item that gives the appearance of, or simulates genital, or buttocks area.

I wish I had gotten this story earlier I would of put it next to the sledding band in Iowa. What is the reason for such a band? Is this about as stupid as the sledding band? What he is really saying is guys can't be outside in public with their shirts off and girls can't show their butts. If we let this go through then you better be prepared for the two piece swimsuit to become extinct.

**What if** we look at how Senator David Moore grew up. Did he run around without a shirt on when he was younger? Are we not going overboard in the area of clothing restrictions, A dress code for yoga outfits out in public just seems a little extreme. Everyone knows it is an outfit that makes people look fit.

**What if** we call it sexist due to mostly women wear these outfits? Is this not a form of discrimination attacking just the yoga outfits? If we pay close attention here you will see someone later on pushing this law on the two piece swimsuit, arguing that it falls under this as well.

I know you're wondering why do I even care about some dumb Bill they are trying to pass in Montana. I will tell you why Montana deserves to have the same rights to dress the way they want to just like you and I do.

**What if** we look at this as a violation of freedom of speech, to express yourself through the clothes you wear? I am all for less restrictions by the government to sensitize our freedoms, while at the same time all about us being held accountable for our own actions.

If we are going to try and pass some Bills let's make them good ones that we can be proud we're passing on to our children and their children.
Since this story came out in the news, the Senator has since corrected his statement saying it was all a joke. Let's get serious America needs us to stay on task.

# A dangerous gray area

A middle school in Pennsylvania is under fire by parents who want to know who passed out cross words from the movie *Fifty Shades of Grey.* Officials in the Monessen School District said they don't know who passed out the puzzles to an unknown number of students, according to the Associated Press.
Words like spanking, bondage, submissive, leather cuffs and other words more offensive. To the parents they want to know why a school would subject their students and our kids to this?

 James Carter one of the parents, said he tried questioning the school's principal and dean of students, but they stopped talking once he insisted on recording the conversation. Superintendent Leanne Spazak said the incident was being investigated.

**What if** we start looking at our schools closer, it seems there are way too many things that are popping up that no one wants to take credit for. I am sure many of our schools are being run just fine, while there are still others that leave much doubt. It is us parents that have to make sure we are staying aware of what goes on in the schools, for our kids sake as well as the communities. When a supervisor stops talking only makes him look guilty. Why would he not want to stand alongside the parents, fighting **this battle** with them?

# Puerto Rico and the United States

Legislators in Puerto Rico are debating a bill that would fine parents of obese children up to $800 if they don't lose weight. The bill aims to improve children's wellbeing and help parents make healthier choices, Sen. Gilberto Rodriguez stated, according to the Associated Press.

 If this gets approved public school teachers would be responsible for flagging obesity cases that they deemed appropriate to the counselors or health department. They would then look at meeting with the parents to determine if the obesity is a result of pour eating habits or a medical condition. They also would create a diet-and-exercise program combined with monthly visits to ensure it's being followed.

**What if** I told you this sounds really close to Michelle Obama's *Let's Move* program. I know there is no $800.00 fine but no reason for a fine when you already implemented your program into the schools where the parents and kids don't get a choice, or say in what they think may be best.

I understand Puerto Rico is not part of the United States, but we do have one thing in common families being told how to raise our children by our governments.

# Girl Scout leader not listening

A mother of an eight year old girl has accused the Girl Scouts of discrimination with her daughter who is deaf.

A Florida mom Sloan LoSauro says she wanted Vanessa, Her daughter, to be a Girl Scout because she thought "it would be good for her to get in with a group of girls and learn the ropes of life," she tells Yahoo Parenting. "I wanted her to learn the things that the Girl Scouts teach you – to honor, to respect, to raise money for others."

Today, there are 2.8 million Girl Scouts—2 million girl members and 800,000 adult members working primarily as volunteers. This is according to the Girl Scouts home page.

The troop leader would not accept Vanessa into their organization and told the mother she could possibly open up a Girl Scout for the deaf.

**What if** we look at the motto of the Girl Scouts?

In Girl Scouts, girls discover the fun, friendship, and power of girls together. Through a myriad of enriching experiences, such as extraordinary field trips, sports skill-building clinics, community service projects, cultural exchanges, and environmental stewardships, girls grow courageous and strong. Girl Scouting helps girls develop their full individual potential; relate to others with increasing understanding, skill, and respect;

develop values to guide their actions and provide the foundation for sound decision-making; and contribute to the improvement of society through their abilities, leadership skills, and cooperation with others.

**What if** we get real here, are they saying deaf girls can't have fun discovering new things and meeting new people their age? Are they saying deaf people can't learn to adjust and cope through a myriad of games and activities? Are they saying they only want to associate with a select few that are not handicapped.

**What if** we look at the founder of the Girl Scouts. I wonder how she would feel knowing a young girl was turned away due to a hearing impairment?

Juliette Gordon Low, founder of Girl Scouts of the USA, was born Juliette Magill Kinzie Gordon on October 31, 1860, in Savannah, Georgia.

Before her marriage, Juliette had suffered from chronic ear infections. She had lost most of her hearing in one ear because of improper treatment. At her wedding, when she was 26, she lost hearing in her other ear after a grain of good-luck rice thrown at the event lodged in her ear, puncturing the eardrum and resulting in an infection and total loss of hearing in that ear.

What if we suspend those who think they are too good to help others, especially an organization that to some see the girls as a ploy to exploit others out of money using the sweetness of a child's innocents for a company's own gain.

What if the next time they come to your door to sell cookies you tell them you only buy from the deaf. I can only hope this is an isolated incident, I hate the thought of no more thin mints.

## Obama Selfie add

At a time where terrorism is at its highest, when an American woman is killed, then flaunted by Isis, Isil, Radical Islamist, or the misguided Easterner, which ever name you chose to use. Our President Barrack Obama once again focuses on the one instead of the many, as he takes pictures of himself in an add on TV, rather than deal with the problems of the world that we all voted him into office to do. Less than twenty four hours had passed and he was doing an add when he should have been rallying for some American justice for the death of Kayla Mueller.

When will America wake up and see that Obama doesn't care about America, if he does, at best he is only half a President.

He doesn't seem to grasp the severity of his own actions and how the world views him. Maybe he does but chooses to ignore the rest of the world thinking he is all that matters.

How disrespectful could one be who is to lead our country, yet focuses only on himself, even in a light hearted sense, when knowingly he turns away from true crisis's and our allies in a time of need.

I think Global warming could wait till we get our terrorist activities in order, let's prioritize. I understand I am only a Sofa Sergeant and he out ranks me, but I still have an opinion. Our country is turning from steel into aluminum. We have become softer, more flexible and unreliable when the heat is on.

The only thing I got out of the Obama selfie add was him trying to stick his cookie into his glass knowing it wouldn't work and it not working. It to me was a parody to how he expects to fight the war on terror without naming the enemy, there is no one to fight.

**Let our flag that waves up above, keep her dignity, as we humble her from below.**

# <u>Change of Menu</u>

There's one troop of young girls in Oakland that discusses matters of racial inequality and wear brown berets. Their organization is called the Radical Brownies. All the members are girls of color or mixed-race. The Radical Brownies are not affiliated with the Girl Scouts of the USA.

Radical Brownies is dedicated to providing young girls of color relevant life experiences, explains the group's co-founder Anayvette Martinez. Martinez, a community organizer, created the Radical Brownies with Marilyn Hollinquest because "there aren't enough spaces [for young girls of color] in our society." In the Radical Brownies, girls learn about social justice movements such the Black Panthers and the Chicano group Brown Berets. They wear their brown berets in homage to those two groups. The Black Panthers are known for their violence. They believed Martin Luther King JR's none violent approach had failed.

**What if** we look at why someone would subject kids to a club that was identified as violent?

What is an eight year old going to know about equality when they themselves are just a kid? Does this not fall into a gray area, that we may call a hate crime. Here you are educating kids by separating them emotionally and physically by color. Does this not fall in under child abuse?

**What if** we taught love and forgiveness, instead of hate and vengeance. Who should we hold accountable when the next reign of terror comes from our children? Something to think about in the drug world kids are used to transport the drugs to protect the dealers from doing time, so is it not something to take a look at when it comes to recruiting young girls for a cause, or cause and effect?

Is this group willing to share their views in a peaceful manner so as all can grow together or are they more interested in trying to pass the Caucasian in every aspect? Maybe I am just not clear on what their true intensions are when you talk equality but only are willing to look at the colors needs.

# <u>Guilty</u>

In Chapel hill North Carolina near the University three Muslims were allegedly gunned down by a neighbor over a parking dispute. It's currently under investigation like any other crime scene would be and should be. Relatives of the victims are wanting it to be seen as a hate crime.

Obama has made his first comments about the three young Muslims who were shot to death in North Carolina saying, "No one in America should ever be targeted "because of who they are, what they look like or how they worship." Here we go again he is sending a message about racism using those words above. No one has even completed an investigation yet and here is Mr. President Obama trying to influence the world through the media and propaganda. Deah Shaddy Barakat twenty three, Yusor Mohammad twenty one and Razan Mohammad Abu-Salha nineteen. I am just waiting on President Obama to say these could have been his kids or another way of saying, this could have been him thirty years ago.

# <u>Rice Reality</u>

Susan Rice is the National Security Advisor and was quoted as saying the following on national TV.

"While The dangers we face may be more numerous and varied, they are not of the existential that we confronted during World War II, or during the Cold War. We cannot afford to be buffeted by alarmism and a nearly instantaneous news cycle."

Let's look at this closer. May be more numerous, means more often. Varied to incorporate a variety of different ways or means, which we call terrorism. Existential means concerned with existence, especially human existence.

For being the National Security Advisor she is way off the mark. I get in her fancy translation of words that, although we may be experiencing more attacks, it's just a few people at a time that are dying verses a larger amount as in World War II. They want to blame the media for over reacting, yet they are the ones using the media to manipulate and minimize all the terror that is going on in the world. She forgets to mention in World War II we were not fighting here but there. I will give her credit she has been the perfect captain that is willing to go down with her ship the USS White House.

# CHAPTER NINE

## The Armed Services.

The Marine Corps was founded in 1775 in Tun Tavern Pennsylvania. To be the best the few, the proud, the Marines Not everyone can be one and some choose to go a different path, but those that chose the elite way to serve are forever forged as Devil Dogs.

Yes I am proud to be one. To those that chose the Army, Navy, Air Force, or Coast Guard I am proud to call you my brothers and sisters. In the military we all have our battles and competitions among each other, but we are all Americans first. We stand united to fight for this glorious nation of ours. To protect her from harm's way, both foreign and domestic.

The Red, White and Blue stand for Freedom and Justice, this was not given to us, but earned through countless battles, that our ancestors fought for their families and ours.

President Obama is at present the Commander and Chief. He wears our uniform as well. I only hope he understands how his position effects all of us, those that are currently serving and those that have served, to those that will someday serve.

We can thank all our organizations like the American Legion, Veteran of Foreign Wars, Red Cross, Daughters of American Revolution, The National Rifle Association and many more.

This book was written with one purpose in mind to bring everything out in the open, to be transparent as President Obama would say.

I am sure there will be some who disagree with my thoughts. I respect their opinions as they should respect mine. All I ask is that you look at each topic openly and fairly, the final decision is yours.

No one in this book is charged with a crime other than through the Authors opinions. Like I had mentioned earlier if your name appears in this book you are not guilty or innocent, you just happen to fall in under the **What if** factor.

# A Proud American

An American I am proud to be
To live safely in this country
Let no one alone or united
Attack our home and try to divide it

For those that try
And that's your choice
Expect to die
Now hear our voice

We united will always stand
To protect this great land
So lower your flags of black and white
Or Red, White and Blue will come and fight

# ABOUT THE AUTHOR

Timothy J. Amdahl grew up in a small town, called Estherville, Iowa. He graduated in 1981 and served two years with the Army and then transferred in to the United States Marine Corps. He was honorably discharged in 1987 after serving four and a half years in the Marine Corps. He has worked as a youth counselor for four years helping the children of our future.

He is married with four children and is currently working for the Illinois Department of Corrections as a Correctional officer, having already served fourteen years. He is a proud American who only wishes to unite our country once again in these troubling times.

**What if** is a book he created to help others slow down and look at where our country is headed. If nothing else to bring us all together to debate the **"What if's"** so that the future can and will change for the better.

He would like to thank all the Americans once again for their contribution to our country and thank all of you for contributing to this book and taking the time to read it.


**Let us make America once again strong.**